The Thousand Year Company

The Thousand Year Company

Anton G Camarota PhD

Acknowledgement

would like to thank Mariko Okada, Makoto Kanda, Ichiro Okada, John Harten, and Yuji Fukazawa for their assistance in completing this book.

Table of Contents

Table of Figures

Table of Tables

"We have lived our lives by the assumption that what was good for us would be good for the world. We have been wrong. We must change our lives so that it will be possible to live by the contrary assumption, that what is good for the world will be good for us. And that requires that we make the effort to know the world and learn what is good for it."

— Wendell Berry, *The Long-Legged House*

Preface

The morning is exceptionally quiet. As I turn on the light and walk across the room, several black widow spiders scurry back through the cracks in the bamboo celling, clinging to their silken webs. There is no sound save for the gurgling of the flowing springs and the cry of a single bird far down the canyon.

First light has just begun to softly illuminate the clouds that float through the valley. Across the way, a stand of tall red cedars, their fragrance wafting across the dell, guard the ancient spring. I can barely make out the deep red of their trunks through the dense branches.

The water seems to laugh and speak, and I soon realize that these waters have flowed in much the same manner for centuries. As I sink into the wooden tub and the water's warmth spreads through me, I feel its restorative power as countless people have done before me.

I am lost in time, entertaining visions of samurai and emperors, of monks and common folk, all seeking the curative energy of the springs. I am deep in the mountains of Japan, far from the noise and bustle of the overcrowded cities, surrounded by the quiet of the forest. Here the natural world has been preserved and protected and the precious waters of Keiunkan continue to flow.

As the eras passed and as civilizations rose and fell, as wars were fought and fortunes shifted, and as shoguns, emperors, kings and queens gained and then lost their empires, these waters have flowed. Through the centuries, the modest yet unceasing efforts of the Fukuzawa family have preserved this place, along the way creating what is now the world's longest-lived business.

I think of the emerging trend of sustainability in business today, and the profusion of strategies managers have implemented that claim to offer meaningful results. Scholars across the globe have produced hundreds of theories about what makes a business sustainable. Yet it seems that these efforts have failed to protect the future of human beings and the planet Earth. Modern industrial organizations are continuing to deplete natural resources on a vast scale and are generating millions of tons of toxic wastes. Their continued actions are endangering both the long-term future of the Earth's living systems as well as the ability of future generations of humans to exist and flourish.

There is, however, a select group of businesses that are examples of sustainable operations, one of which is providing the experience in which I am immersed. These companies have managed to endure and thrive through several ages of man – tribal, feudal, industrial, and now the information age. Despite major social changes, these businesses have remained viable by making positive contributions to their employees, their customers, and their stakeholders, including the natural environment. They are living examples of what really works for sustainability.

Just as with the apocryphal story of the man who is looking for his lost keys outside of his house under the streetlight instead of inside the darkened house where he lost them, most business leaders have been looking for answers to the sustainability dilemma in the wrong place. Seeking answers for how to develop a successful sustainability strategy within the contemporary industrial-age worldview is destined to fail – the answers will simply not be found within a set of Cartesian assumptions. Truly viable sustainability strategies can be found only by examining the operations of very long-lived companies. Such examinations can help contemporary leaders to develop a different understanding of how long-lived companies have survived and prospered over time, which in turn will enable leaders to implement strategies that result in a truly sustainable business.

For a business to endure, thrive, and sustain itself no matter what changes happen in human society, it must embody the essence and deepest meaning of sustainability. Such embodiment can be found in Keiunkan, a company that has existed for more than 1300 years. Throughout the centuries, this humble inn has kept going, providing a unique atmosphere and a special place for all visitors.

More than merely surviving, longevity is also about thriving. Exemplifying the acumen engendered through hundreds of years of practice – a respect for traditions, an astute awareness of the present, and a commitment to endurance – the very old companies throughout the world are models of what is possible. Along with Keiunkan, they are living tributes to the wisdom and significance of operational longevity. Rooted in both harmony with the environment and a respect for life, they show us the way to towards a positive future that is truly sustainable.

Introduction

magine, if you will, that you are a manager or an employee of a company that has existed for not one hundred, not five hundred, but for more than a thousand years. What would your daily life as a manager be like? How would you embody the company traditions and seek operational excellence? What would be the core values that guide you in your daily activities? And most important, how would you help the company to not only survive, but flourish in the coming centuries?

Such a company actually exists. This book introduces the Nishiyama Keiunkan Onsen, the world's longest-lived company. It defines the exemplary management practices and leadership behaviors that have enabled the company to thrive for more than 1300 years despite the radical changes in the world, including the transition from monarchy to feudalism and then to industrialism, several world wars, and finally the transformation of industrialism and the onset of the information age. The leadership and management practices of the company illustrate how Keiunkan has defied the odds and managed to thrive over the millennia.

Keiunkan is not alone. There are many companies throughout the world that have been in operations for centuries. The Weltenberger Kloster brewery in Regensburg, Germany, has been brewing beer continually since 1050 AD. Their beer is of the highest quality and won the World Beer Cup Gold Award in 2004, 2008, and 2012. Similarly, the Barone Ricasoli winery near Castelnuovo Berardenga in Italy has been making Chianti since 1584, and this wine was recently chosen as one of the best 100 wines in the world. The Brazen Head pub in Dublin, Ireland, has been serving its customers the finest food and libations since 1198 AD.

These examples and those of many other similar long-lived companies are the basis of the management framework in this book. They serve as models for what it takes to operate a sustainable business: one that starts, succeeds, and continues to be successful over time.

A central idea of this book is that if a company has managed to maintain its operations for centuries, it is by definition sustainable. In support of this idea, in this book you will find many important insights and explanations of strategies that long-lived businesses have implemented, as well as the principles applied to achieve exemplary performance. Finally, you will discover an integrated sustainability framework that you can adopt for your organization, no matter what industry, company size, or existing business you are in.

The problem of business sustainability is painted in broad strokes, presenting an overall philosophy of sustainable business for leaders and managers to take on and make their own. Such a broad approach requires that you think critically about how you can adapt the philosophy to fit your specific business context. Although there are examples of solutions that have worked for Keiunkan and for other long-lived businesses, each reader should use the Thousand Year Model as the starting point for developing their own processes and systems that fit their specific business.

In other words, for those interested in sustainability, this book is about what needs to be done and why it is important – not the specific way to do it. There is no silver bullet or instantaneous fix. Readers interested in building a long-lived and sustainable company must determine for themselves how to go about implementing the leadership principles and management priorities in the best ways possible. The core of the book is The Thousand Year Model, which sets the framework for a comprehensive and integrated set of operating principles that illustrate Keiunkan's operations. These principles have worked to enable Keiunkan to be successful for more than a thousand years, and yet they can be applied in any business today and customized to meet the specific needs of any product or service.

Who this book is for

This book is for leaders and managers who think that operating a business over the long term is important, and that finding one's own approaches for leading and managing sustainably is the best way to proceed. This book is also for entrepreneurs who want to build their company so that it can endure the changes that will cause competitors to shutter their operations. Throughout this book, you will discover the management secrets that have enabled Keiunkan to sustain their operations, thrive, and flourish over the centuries. If you are interested in helping your company to be more effective at sustaining operations over time, this book is for you.

In short, this book is for:

- Executive managers who would like to increase the resilience of their company, develop its ability to operate sustainably, and learn how to withstand severe change
- Operational managers who would like to increase the effectiveness of their management systems in meeting strategic goals
- Employees who would like to gain a deeper understanding of leadership and management for longevity
- Students in the field of sustainability management who want to increase their knowledge of effective leadership approaches.

Why you should read this book

No matter what industry you are in, you will find ideas and concepts applicable to your business. Even if you are in a government or non-governmental organization, you can find value in the strategies presented. Supporting examples come from the operations of Keiunkan and other companies, and illustrate specific businesses solutions to the paradoxes and challenges inherent in managing for the long term. These examples reveal why and how the company has managed to remain a viable enterprise century after century.

But perhaps the most important reason for reading this book is survivability. In a turbulent era marked by both great change and high failure rates for most companies, it is relatively easy for businesses to lose their focus and vanish. The example of Keiunkan can motivate and inspire us to pursue longevity as a core business objective. As economic fortunes boom and wane, companies embracing resilience will remain steadfast and true to their credos, making meaningful positive contributions to the world over extended periods of time and thus serving as examples for others.

Readers of this book can expect to:

- Understand a robust framework for strategic longevity management
- Distinguish different principles for building organizational resilience and sustainability

- Comprehend ways to make their companies more effective at continuing operations over time
- Gain clarity on how their business meets the needs of their customers and other stakeholders
- Interpret the Thousand Year Model in a way that can be applied meaningfully to their business
- Extend their knowledge of management and leadership methods based on what has worked for hundreds of years
- Identify areas where their companies might improve the quality of their contributions to the world

How this book is organized

Chapter 1 of this book is the history of Nishiyama Keiunkan Onsen, which has been featured in the Guinness Book of World Records as the world's oldest company. An overview of the company's operations and the context for the factors that have affected its longevity are provided. Chapter 2 delves into the idea of what a sustainable business is and what it must do to remain viable, and defines the principles of the Thousand Year Model. Chapter 3 describes the critically important role of leadership and why skilled leaders are necessary for an organization's long-term success. Chapter 4 defines each management element of the Thousand Year Model and explains the activities necessary for managing sustainable operations. Finally, Chapter 5 closes with a hopeful message about the future, and suggests both a philosophy and a practical approach that can help the next generation of businesses to become sustainable. Throughout the book are examples of how the leadership and management practices of Keiunkan and other companies hew to the Thousand Year Model, and how they have formed the basis for their success.

CHAPTER 1

The Keiunkan Story

Origins

Many years ago in Japan, Fujiwara Masato was wandering high in the mountains hunting for food. With his joints aching from the cold, he struggled to move through the dense pine and cedar forests. After a strenuous day trudging through the forested hills, he lay down on his mat, spent and stiff. Drifting off into a troubled sleep, he had a vivid dream of a strange creature that spoke to him of a place of warmth, and pointed the way through the forest.

The next day, having awoken with the dream still clear in his mind, he began his hunting anew. As he walked, he realized he was following a path just like the one in his dream. It wound through a valley to a small clearing where the Hayakawa and Yukawa rivers met. On the banks of the Yukawa River, Masato discovered a fountain of hot water spouting vigorously among the rocks just as the creature in his dream had shown him. He decided to soak his aching body, and found that his stiffness vanished as the spring rejuvenated him.

Masato stayed in the spot for many weeks, and dug a small space among the rocks where he could soak his entire body. His limbs now nimble and his vitality restored, he stayed in the area for some time, drinking the water and making day trips to hunt. On one of his trips, he wandered into a nearby settlement where he told the villagers of the spring. The villagers began to journey to the spring, where they rested and allowed the waters to restore them. The spring became known in the local communities as a place of health.

Many years later, Emperor Mommu looked out about his realm with concern. Much of the country was lawless and in disarray, and many chieftains were fighting for control of land, crops, and villages. Emperor Mommu appointed Fuhito Fujiwara to write a set of laws that would bring the country together into a set of provinces, districts, townships, and neighborhoods. In order to administer the realm, the emperor needed a complete list of all the towns and villages as well as a recent map of the country. Emperor Mommu commanded Fuhito to journey throughout the country and gather up all of the information he could find about how many people were living in different areas and what they were engaged in as part of their daily lives. Fuhito set out to fulfill the emperor's commands and began a journey far and wide throughout the land. The year was 704 A.D.

Almost a year later, on a very cold and cloudy night, Fuhito Fujiwara walked into the town of Hayakawa. Tired from his journey and weak from a steady diet of only rice, he sought lodging for the evening. The local people provided a room in a small house and told him about a place that could help him restore his energy. Fuhito decided to visit the spring. He had traveled for many months, but he still had many more to go. The next day, Fuhito set out walking upstream for several miles along the banks of the Hayakawa river until he noticed a plume of steam rising from a small pool of warm water along a rock outcropping. Feeling tired and spent from his long journey from Kyoto, he sank into the warm waters and immediately felt refreshed.

Fuhito noticed a small house that the local Fukazawa family had built as a place of rest for travelers and local villagers. He rose from the spring feeling better than he had in many weeks and walked up to the house and inquired of its residents. Greeting him warmly, the head of the family invited Fuhito to stay the night and join them for the evening meal. Fuhito assented, and stayed for several days, regaining his strength and becoming friends with the Fukuzawa family. Impressed by their hospitality, the power of the water, and the seclusion of the mountains, Fuhito in his official capacity as a court noble declared that the Fukuzawa family owned the property, and thus by official decree the *onsen* (hot spring) was founded. The year was 705 AD.

Figure 1. The original hot spring location from 705 AD

When Fuhito returned to the palace in Kyoto, word spread about the waters in the Minami Alps, and the royal family made several journeys there. In 718 AD, the high priests of the capital set out on their own journeys to establish temples throughout the land, stopping often at the Fukuzawa onsen. Over time, more and more people sought out the spring as a place to restore their vitality. These journeys, taken by nobleman and commoners alike, became the stuff of legend, and for the next several hundred years, emperors, shoguns, samurai warriors, priests, and commoners continued to make pilgrimages to the springs. These journeys instilled the tradition of visiting the onsen deeply into Japanese culture.

Figure 2. Hayakawa River Valley as it might have appeared in 705 AD

The Onsen Today

The place Fuhito helped found is today known as the Nishiyama Keiunkan Onsen, a hot springs inn located deep in the mountains of Japan. Situated on a steep hillside high in the Minami Alps, Keiunkan is a place of restoration and relaxation for all who visit. Underneath the inn flows the Hayakawa River, whose headwaters begin several miles further up the valley. Starting as a trickle on the flanks of the soaring 10,474 foot-high Kita Peak, the Hayakawa River gradually swells and grows in size and volume as it dances down the valley. Many miles later at the town of Minobu, it joins the Fuji River where it completes its journey past Mt. Fuji to the sea.

The waters of the Hayakawa River originate from both above and under the ground. As the river descends from Kita Peak, a series of underground springs bubble up and merge with the river. This part of Japan is a volcanic region, and the river runs along a seam where the North American and Eurasian tectonic plates meet. Water

4

hitting the magma close to the Earth's core is heated and finds its way up through the seam to the surface, where it emerges at several locations to join the flowing river. It is the largest of these underground springs that is at the heart of the Keiunkan onsen.

The purity of the inn's water is at its core of service-value provision. The water emerges untreated from an underground source at 125 degrees Fahrenheit, the perfect temperature for soaking. Due to numerous natural purification processes that have taken place deep within the Earth, the water is absolutely safe for drinking, and many visitors take home large quantities to enjoy after their visit. Before the advent of modern medicine, the many thousands who made the arduous journey up the Hayakawa River valley believed that the water had the power to heal ills and cure diseases.

Over the centuries, the Nishiyama Keiunkan Onsen has continued to be a popular destination for people to come for rest and relaxation. Amazingly, the Fukazawa family has maintained ownership in a continuous line of succession up until the present day, for over 1300 successive years. This is a world record that has been verified by the *Guinness Book of World Records*: Nishiyama Keiunkan Onsen is the oldest hotel in existence, in continuous operation since 705 AD. Such longevity can serve as a source of inspiration to today's business leaders.

Yuji Fukazawa, the current CEO and owner, is the 52nd generation of family to operate the inn. He has presided over the inn's restoration since 1975, transforming it from an older-style wooden structure to a modern luxury hotel. Its size has roughly doubled since then, to its current thirty-seven rooms, and the menu has been revised to include only local foods of the highest possible quality. Each of the rooms has a view of the tranquil and relaxing landscapes that surround the inn.

The hotel has withstood many challenges over its lifetime. Being located on a mountainside means that mudslides are a frequent occurrence, as are floods from the river. Several times, large portions of the hotel have been damaged or washed away only to be rebuilt again with improved style and strength, eventually transitioning from wood to a stronger and safer concrete structure. The road to the inn is frequently closed due to rock falls and washouts, yet even with these travel difficulties, the inn remains at an 80% occupancy throughout the year, with greater than a 40% return rate for loyal customers. Not bad for an inn that charges more than $450 per room per night.

Figure 3. Greeting the visitor

How has the inn kept up its continuous operations for more than 1300 years? According to Yuji Fukazawa, the management's approach is very simple, yet very effective: easy to state but hard to implement, including the following:

- A relentless and uncompromising focus on quality, centered on (a) continual improvement of customer satisfaction, and, (b) performance excellence
- A respect for tradition combined with a willingness to experiment with new ways of enhancing the guest experience
- The nurturing of imagination and creativity when innovating new ways to serve the guests
- The provision of superior customer value, even at more than $450 per night per room
- The development of personal connections with every guest
- Serving a niche of discerning customers that have high personal standards for lodging and service
- The selection and development of a superior staff
- Emphasizing employee satisfaction first, and acknowledging this as the driver of customer satisfaction

- Creating a business setting that instills pride in employees
- The preservation of the core technology (the pure hot springs water and the natural environment surrounding the inn)
- Integrating the inn with its natural environment
- The maintenance of an atmosphere of remoteness, quiet, and peace
- The linkage of the inn's services to the cultural values of Japanese society as well as the personal needs of guests
- The implementation of strong cost controls over all phases of operations – food, facilities, a tunnel for local highways, and employees
- The provision for lengthy project planning combined with a rapid decision making process for important milestone decisions
- The integration of the inn with the local economy by purchasing the restaurant food from local farms
- Contributing positively to the local community

These strategies have been refined continually throughout the centuries and implemented by successive generations of management. While the owners have provided strategic direction, the on-site managers have supervised daily operations and ensured that employees were available to meet all of the operating requirements for the inn. Keiunkan has survived every revolution in Japanese society, and has successfully weathered the changes from feudalism to monarchy, from monarchy to democracy, the closing of the entire country to outsiders for 200 years, a destructive war that leveled the major cities of the country, and the transitions from an agrarian to an industrial economy, and then to today's informational economy. Amazingly, through all of these changes, the inn has not only survived; it has thrived, and has become a keeper of core cultural values as well.

Keiunkan's dedication to sustainability, excellence, and continual improvement is an example of what can be accomplished through steadfast leadership and the right long-term strategies. The inn is an example of a truly sustainable business that holds the triple bottom line of people, profits, and planet at the core of its business model. All facets of the inn's operation contribute to its longevity, and enhance its value not only as a mountain destination, but also as a cultural icon. Firmly anchored in the natural environment, the inn's leaders are dedicated to preserving the precious waters that flow from beneath its lands. Throughout the centuries since its founding, the inn's managers have maintained a singular focus on enabling travelers from all over Japan to experience the restorative powers of the natural volcanic waters of the Minami Alps. It is this focus that is at the heart of Keiunkan's operations.

Figure 4. Nishiyama Keiunkan Onsen as it appears today

CHAPTER 2

Understanding Sustainability Management

For years, I have been researching sustainability and sustainability management, and have been working on discovering what a truly sustainable business looks like. I have tracked the development of strategies such as green management, technical reporting, management systems, renewable energy, and performance improvement. Although these approaches seem hopeful, the widespread industrialization of societies throughout the world has continued to deplete resources and decrease human wellbeing.

Sustainability management has faced a seemingly unsolvable paradox: while employee productivity has increased exponentially during the past thirty years, median income has dropped, job satisfaction has decreased, and both the economic status and social wellbeing of many employees have declined. Along with these changes, almost all businesses have increased both their use of natural resources and generation of wastes, and have found it difficult to convert the general principle of sustainability into specific business operations. As Matthew Tueth, the Steelcase Foundation Professor of Sustainable Business at Aquinas College says, "Our conventional approaches for producing goods and services routinely include unnecessarily insidious and tragic consequences for future generations of all life."

Yet on my trips to Japan I have encountered companies whose operations seemed to fly in the face of this assessment. These companies are known collectively as *shinise*, or "very old businesses." Such establishments are found throughout the country. During a visit to a pickle factory that has been operating successfully for more than

300 years, I suddenly realized that these very old companies had solved the sustainability paradox. Not only have these companies thrived for centuries, their employees have remained happy and productive, and their technologies have been continually updated to maintain the highest possible quality of products and services. I resolved then and there to study how these companies were managed so successfully, and how they had flourished over hundreds of years and successive generations.

The result of this study is The Thousand Year Model of sustainability management, which is introduced in this chapter. By reviewing the elements of this model, managers can gain a deeper understanding of how to build an organization that can survive change, be resilient in the face of difficulties, and continue to exist in the face of seemingly insurmountable odds. It's important to note that, in most cases, the odds are only *seemingly* insurmountable. As Keiunkan and other companies have shown, with the right model, time is no barrier to success. The Thousand Year Model can be applied to any organization in any industry. The principles it contains have been proven by not only Keiunkan, but also by hundreds of long-lived companies throughout the world, some of which are shown in Appendix A. Those companies that have implemented the elements of the Thousand Year Model have not only survived, but have flourished over the centuries.

Business Failure – and Success

One of the unchanging facts about new businesses is that most startup companies will fail, and the high failure rates of startup businesses are well known. In addition, most business, regardless of how successful they are, do not last very long. According to Arie de Geus:

> The average life expectancy of a multinational corporation – Fortune 500 or its equivalent – is between forty and fifty years... A full one-third of the companies listed in the 1970 Fortune 500, for instance, had vanished by 1983 – acquired, merged, or broken to pieces... In some countries, 40 percent of all newly created companies last less than ten years. A recent study by Ellen de Rooij of the Stratix Group in Amsterdam indicates that the average life expectancy of all firms, regardless of size, measured in Japan and much of Europe, is only 12.5 years.

The failure rate among family-owned businesses is much the same. According to William O'Hara, author of the book *Centuries of Success*,

*Between the first and second generations, only about one third of family busi-
nesses survive and, of those survivors, only approximately 12 percent reach a
third generation. An exclusive 3 to 4 percent of third generation survivors make
it to a fourth.*

When we consider these figures, we see that 99.85% of all startup businesses will not
make it beyond the eighty-year mark. According to Leslie Hannah at the University of
Tokyo, the average half-life of the top 100 companies by market capitalization is seven-
ty-five years. The US Bureau of Labor Statistics has stated that 50-60% of all businesses
fail in the first five years, and 75% of all businesses fail within ten years. According to
the US Census Bureau, of the top twenty-five industrial corporations in the United
States in 1900, only two remained on that list at the start of the 1960s. Of the top
twenty-five companies in the Fortune 500 in 1961, only six remain there today. Stacy
Perman, an award-winning journalist for BusinessWeek and the author of three books,
has found a similar situation with family-owned businesses: 30% of family-owned
businesses make it to the second generation, 3.6% of family-owned businesses make
it to the third generation, and only 0.12% of family-owned businesses make it to the
fourth generation. These rates of business failure are shown in Figure 5.

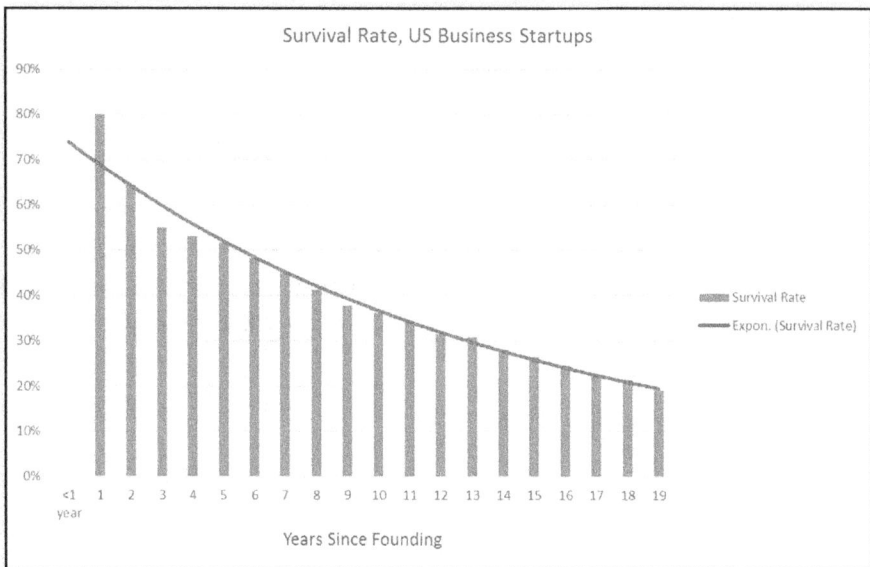

Figure 5. US business survival rates

In stark contrast to all of these failures is a group of companies that defy the failure rates, such as Keiunkan. These companies are located throughout the world, and have managed to not only avoid self-destructing, but instead have thrived despite the odds for centuries. These companies have shown what it means to be sustainable – they are examples of organizations that have adapted to sometimes radical changes that caused lesser companies to vanish, and that have shown their resilience in the face of seemingly overwhelming catastrophes. To understand why Keiunkan has been so successful over time and how any company can become more sustainable and build for the long term, the priorities and strategies for long-term success are described below. These approaches help explain how long-lived companies have maintained their competitive edge for centuries, and can become models for sustainability management.

The Concept of Sustainability

Unfortunately, the terms "sustainability" and "sustainability management" have been overused to the point of becoming almost meaningless. One of the most confusing aspects of these terms is that they can have multiple meanings in different contexts, some of which are even opposed to one another. For the purposes of this book, we will sketch out the characteristics of a sustainable business organization by using the Thousand Year Model, and establish the meaning of sustainability in the context of leading and managing primarily via the example of the longest-lived company – Keiunkan.

The first characteristic of sustainability is that **it is both a goal and a process.** It can be viewed as the capacity of a company to endure changes over time, and the ability to maintain its operations at an optimal level throughout extended intervals. As a goal, sustainability is held by leaders as a core decision criterion and a highly desired outcome. As a process, sustainability is about maintaining productive activities over time in the most efficient ways possible. We can formally define these two aspects of sustainability as follows:

Sustainability as a Goal

A sustainable company is dedicated to living together well, flourishing, and creating a positive influence on the world.

Sustainability as a Process

A sustainable company develops and maintains the capacity to endure changes in its operating environment by renewing and restoring the resources essential for its operations indefinitely.

The importance of this first distinction is that **sustainability requires both management and leadership.** If either is missing, an organization will simply not be able to maintain its operations over time. When we view sustainability as a goal, it becomes the job of leaders to define what this goal means for the organization and to align the different organizational functions so that the goal is achieved. When we view sustainability as a process, it becomes the job of managers to plan, organize, and staff the systems necessary to achieve the goal.

The second characteristic of sustainability is that it is a **multi-faceted concept.** A sustainable company preserves the integrity of its social, economic, ecological, and technological capital by investing in the development of each form. The core problem for sustainability managers is to optimize these different forms of capital simultaneously. An organization that focuses on optimizing a single form of capital will not long remain in business, as the risks from changes in the other forms of capital will soon be realized. Each of the forms of capital – economic, social, ecological, and technological – is managed in one or more elements of the Thousand Year Model, which in turn are considered together as part of an overall sustainability orientation. The inclusion of the different forms of capital into the Thousand Year Model is shown below in Table 1.

Form of Capital	Currency/ Measure	Key Sustainability Management Concerns	Thousand Year Model Elements
Economic (money-based income)	Money/price	• Optimal compensation distribution • Adequate cash flow • Appropriate size • Operational efficiency	• Control • Commitment & Change
Social (the institutions, relationships, and norms that shape the quality and quantity of a society's social interactions)	Relationships/ significance	• Quality of relationships • Shared value • Modeling the credo • Meeting human needs • Realizing employee potential • Energizing employees • Achieving the mission and purpose	• Mastery • Relationships & Integration • Commitment & Change • Integrity
Technological (non-financial assets used in production)	Knowledge/ productivity	• Quality of products and services • Gaining and applying current scientific knowledge • Quality of stakeholder interactions • Continual improvement	• Learning, • Mastery • Integrity • Commitment & Change
Ecological (ecosystems providing life support)	Life/species richness	• Adaptation to changing ecosystems • Restoration of ecosystem services	• Relationships & Integration • Integrity

Table 1. Integration of Capital Optimization Approach

The third characteristic of sustainability is that it is **concerned with the future of human beings and the planet Earth**. Sustainability is about protecting both the long-term future of the Earth's living systems as well as the ability of future generations of humans to exist and flourish. One of the difficulties of managing for sustainability is that the timeframe for ecological and social change can be several human lifetimes or longer. This means that the impacts of decisions made today will not be experienced for perhaps a hundred years or even longer, and this places a difficult burden on decision makers.

The implication of a future-oriented approach is to create a sense of responsibility for the planet and for unborn generations of people. This sense of responsibility translates into different management approaches for each of the four forms of capital:

- Economic – internalizing and reducing costs previously borne by society
- Social – creation of stable societies based on equitable relationships
- Ecological – preservation of the accumulated knowledge of the past as stored in the world's living systems
- Technological – taking precautionary measures to prevent the possible negative impacts of a technological development before they occur

Although sustainability is a nice idea, unless this idea is translated into practical actions for leaders and managers, it remains just that – a nice idea. Such a translation considers the actions necessary to form a foundation for sustainability management, as well as defines the goal of sustainability for leaders. The seven elements below are common to both Keiunkan as well as other companies such as Avedis Zildjian Company, Confetti Mario Pelino, and Levi Strauss that have remained in continuous existence for 150 years or more.

Sustainability at Keiunkan

We can learn much about how to succeed in the longer term from reviewing Keiunkan's approach to running their organization, which has helped the company to thrive for more than 1300 years. We begin to distinguish the inn's core practices using the following seven elements:

- *Integrity*: the development and maintenance of strong linkages among the organization's purpose, its credo, its brands, its products and services, and its customer experiences
- *Commitment and Change*: the capacity to respond to and shape both external and internal changes
- *Control*: the identification, assessment, and response to uncertainties that affect the achievement of organizational objectives

- *Learning*: the protection of proprietary technology while adapting it to new scientific developments
- *Mastery*: the promotion of employee trust, unity, commitment, involvement, engagement, and enthusiasm
- *Relationships and Connection*: the identification of stakeholder interests and impacts, and the development of strategies to address those interests and impacts
- *Leadership*: the capability of maintaining a long-term focus while balancing the pressing demands of the other six elements

Table 2 provides a brief summary of how the leaders and managers at Keiunkan approach each of the seven elements.

Element	Keiunkan's Actions
Integrity	• Integrating the inn with its natural environment • Maintaining an atmosphere of remoteness, quiet, and peace • Linking the inn's services to the cultural values of Japanese society as well as the personal needs of guests
Commitment and Change	• Preserving the core service technology: the pure hot springs water and the natural environment surrounding the inn • Combining a respect for tradition with a willingness to experiment with new ways of enhancing the guest experience • Nurturing employee imagination and creativity when innovating new ways to serve the guests
Control	• Applying a revenue strategy of premium pricing and high percentage of return guests • Focusing on efficient operations and customer loyalty, not growth • Maintaining a stable size • Compensating employees fairly and at twice the comparable job rate • Keeping fixed costs low • Proactively maintaining the long-term health of the business

Learning	• Focusing relentlessly and uncompromisingly on quality, including (a) continual improvement of customer satisfaction and (b) performance excellence • Balancing tradition with new hotel technologies • Emphasizing the excellence of the core hotel experience • Providing an experience unique in the world, impossible to copy
Mastery	• Hiring employees based on shared values • Managers seek to generate trust and exhibit fairness • Keeping employees on payroll even when productive work is slow • Providing above average compensation • Requiring employees to model core cultural values based on tradition • Requiring extensive socialization and training on all aspects of operations • Placing employees first in all operational decisions • Setting primary operational goals for employee loyalty and retention • Balancing a process and outcome view of the company
Relationships and Connection	• Modeling core cultural values for customers, the community, and the country • Maintaining a strong ecological connection – water is the core of the business • Creating and managing long term customer and supplier relationships • Seeking to provide a net positive stakeholder impact • Seeking to gain a deep understanding of customer needs • Preserving close contact with local communities
Leadership	• Survivability and continuity of the business for the next 1000 years is a prime leadership concern.

Table 2. Summary of Keiunkan's Operational Practices

By looking at any company using this framework, the core success factors become readily apparent. These factors include a core of leadership – the *why* of the company – and the six *hows* of management – in what ways it organizes and controls its operations. One thing is certain: there are drastic differences between conventional management and leadership for longevity. It is these differences that make a difference for both the survival and flourishing of any business, and that form the basis of Keiunkan's success. The following chapters break down each of the seven elements of long-term success, and explore how to use the Thousand Year Model, shown in Figure 6, to take actions that can make your business operate more soundly and thrive over time.

Figure 6. The Thousand Year Model

Commitment & Change

Control

Integrity

Leadership

Integration

Learning

Mastery

CHAPTER 3

Leading a Thousand Year Company

L eadership is at the core of the Thousand Year Model. Without strong and effective leadership, an organization will simply not be able to sustain itself over time. Before any type of management activities are undertaken, leaders must define the company's purpose, the tone of stakeholder relationships, and the time frame within which the company is operating. Absent these criteria, management activities simply do not make any sense, and functional silos as well as political posturing will rise to the fore.

In this book, leadership is defined from an operational standpoint: a focus on what leaders do to make the Thousand Year Model come alive. Rather than traits, skills, or attitudes, we instead focus on the tasks that must be executed in order to sustain a company's operations over time. To begin, sustainability leadership is defined as the following:

> ***Sustainability leadership is the process of interacting with, supporting, influencing, and energizing an organized group of followers to achieve important goals over an extended period of time.***

Since the Thousand Year Model is an operationally-based leadership approach, it is important to begin by defining in more detail exactly what effective leaders do. Understanding what is required of effective sustainability leaders helps us to prepare both ourselves and our companies for implementing the processes and systems necessary for sustainability management. The following sets of activities were first promulgated by Peter Drucker in 2004 and are refined further here to enhance their applicability to a sustainable company.

In a sustainable company, effective leaders perform the following actions:

1. <u>Decide what needs to be done.</u> This involves setting the leadership priorities and determining what can and should be delegated, and what is the right thing that needs to be done for the good of the overall organization.
2. <u>Develop action plans to accomplish what needs to be done.</u> These include commitments to achieve the desired results in all areas of the company, identification of possible barriers and constraints to achieving these results, and implications for the resources required to implement the plans.
3. <u>Take responsibility for decisions.</u> This responsibility includes naming the people both responsible for carrying out the decision results as well as those affected by the decision, the deadline for making the decision, and communicating the decision results to interested parties.
4. <u>Take responsibility for communicating.</u> This responsibility includes sharing the plans with others, gaining feedback on proposed actions, and giving people affected by the action plans the information they need to accomplish their tasks.
5. <u>Focus on opportunities.</u> Sustainability leaders reframe problems and change as opportunities for value enhancement rather than threats to the organization's success. Innovations, changes in industry structure, emerging trends in stakeholder expectations and values, and new scientific knowledge can all be the basis for learning and opportunities to increase shared value.

Although these actions are necessary for effective leadership, they are not sufficient for sustainability leadership. What is missing is the normative component of why the organization exists and what needs it fulfills in the world. While Drucker's recommended actions specify how leaders must function, he does not define the content of their messages to followers nor beliefs about what needs to be done and why it is important.

The Thousand Year Model provides a context within which leaders generate meaning and implement the activities prescribed by Drucker. This framework helps leaders to consider the impacts of decisions throughout a company and develop a more holistic view of their organization's efforts. For example, Drucker states that leaders take responsibility for decisions. In the Thousand Year Model, responsibility for decisions is predicated on gaining information from stakeholders, integrating technology and financial considerations, and reviewing possible impacts on customer experiences. Beyond simply involving the people who are affected by a decision and communicating the results, the Thousand Year Model establishes a normative basis for the criteria that need to be included in any executive-level decision if the organization wishes to sustain its operations.

As a part of this decision-making effort, leaders work within the six management elements of the model to determine where strategies should be developed, enhanced, or implemented, and identify linkages among elements that can be strengthened. Finally, the Thousand Year Model helps leaders to develop an agenda for balancing the driving and restraining forces in a company to ensure the organization's stability and ability to thrive over time. The role of leaders in the Thousand Year Model is shown in Figure 6.

Within the Thousand Year Model, leadership is a unifying force towards a central objective: to influence and energize their organizations to achieve both financial gain and better relationships with people and the natural environment. Leadership touches all elements of the Thousand Year Model, making sure each element is congruent with all of the others while forming important bonds among these elements. Since change is constant, the role of leaders in continually aligning these elements is critical to the success of a sustainable company, and strong bonds make such an alignment possible.

There is also an important implication here: without leadership, a sustainable organization is not possible. When leadership is present and leaders are acting to integrate the elements of the Thousand Year Model, an organization has a fighting chance of remaining viable over time. Without leadership, an organization comes apart as different functions and fiefdoms seek to optimize their bases of power while degrading the performance of the organization as a whole.

The Thousand Year Model is also a framework that resolves the paradox of sustainable operations: constancy of operations can be attained only through continual change. Leaders can use this framework to achieve both dynamic homeostasis and resilience in the face of significant negative events. The Thousand Year Model also offers a strong, well-formed structure that leaders can also use to prevent pressing short-term problems from distracting their attention on what is important for the long-term survival of the business.

The recent example of the collapse of Enron shows clearly how devastating an unwarranted emphasis on short-term actions can be. While the Enron managers thought that they were acting in the best long-term interests of the company, their emphasis on short-term gain destroyed the business. These managers bypassed the financial control and governance systems of the company, deluding both investors and the board of directors with inaccurate earnings figures as well as exhortations that the company was in a solid financial position when it clearly was not. The managers also deceived themselves by thinking that boosting share price using questionable accounting practices was in the long-term interest of the company, when in reality these boosts were driven by the promise of short-term cash bonuses and more stock options for managers. A vicious cycle was created and the financial core of the company was hollowed out. In their drive to build equity, which is a long-term consideration, Enron managers over-emphasized short term actions that ended up costing stakeholders $74 billion dollars.

At the center of the Thousand Year Model is a leadership agenda that is rooted in the meaningfulness of a founder's vision, and which is comprised of five aspects that are essential for leading an organization's operations through successive generations. These aspects, or leadership priorities, can be adopted by multiple generations of leaders. Within each generation, however, the priorities will be actualized in a different manner based on changes in a leader's personal style, emerging social norms, changing ecological conditions, and technological developments.

The five priorities are defined as follows:

1. Purpose: Leaders in a sustainable company define the company's core purpose clearly, and continually reinforce this purpose through modeling values, defining long-term goals, and helping employees to understand the company credo. At Keiunkan, the purpose of the organization is reinforced through Yuji's behaviors, the physical surroundings, and the respect accorded each guest and employee.

2. Adaptation: Leaders in a sustainable company are continually learning about and adapting to changes in stakeholder trends, values, and realities. Adaptation requires being cognizant of the complex interrelationships among the different operational elements of an organization. By maintaining an awareness of and taking actions to respond to changing external conditions, sustainability leaders can ensure the continual supply of resources necessary for the company to function. Yuji's extensive ties to the local community set the groundwork for his adaptive actions.

3. Energy: A core leadership task is to energize and motivate a company's employees. Sustainable company leaders encourage employees to make significant contributions to stakeholder wellbeing, and inform them of the

meaningfulness and importance of their contributions. They do this by reinforcing the company's credo with employees and defining what is true and good. The leader makes sure that the credo, values, and brand resonate with the company's ecological, social, and economic contributions. Yuji manages energy by not only paying his people more than twice the comparable salaries of similar positions, he also selects staff carefully so they have shared values and works with them to reinforce the importance of their work.

4. Time: A sustainable company leader exhibits positive attitudes towards the past history of the company, its mission in the present, and its accountability for the future. These attitudes can be summarized as gratitude for the past, service for the present, and responsibility for the future. The leader creates a sense of both time and place for employees. At Keiunkan, time and place are reinforced by the display of the Guinness World Record certificate along with a display of artifacts from the inn's history.

5. Aesthetics: Sustainability leaders apply a sense of style to the organization's activities based on an aesthetic sensibility developed from both cultural norms and universal principles. Key activities include manipulating symbols and myths, building a desire to belong, and promulgating an atmosphere of pleasurable engagement with organizational activities, products, and services. A sustainability leader will also present themselves to the world as part of an artistic performance that is a creative expression of their inner self as well as a reflection of the prevailing cultural aesthetic. One only has to experience being in Yuji's presence for a short period to appreciate his powerful yet humble bearing, and he has derived the inn's aesthetic from the tight integration of luxury and the natural world.

Each of these priorities involves leaders gaining information from stakeholders, understanding the impacts of this information on the processes within their organizations, and then making decisions about how to implement any necessary changes within an overall sustainability-based framework. The Thousand Year Model offers such a framework and provides a guide to help leaders act on the systems that are most relevant for ensuring organizational survival. These efforts can be complex, and implementation of each of the five core leadership priorities is addressed in more detail in the following sections.

Purpose

At the core of longevity leadership is purpose and meaning. Every business originates with an idea – a reason for starting a business in the first place. This reason is the difference that the founder is attempting to make in the world through their organization. The reason for starting can be considered the business purpose, which is the essence of why the company was created and defines a path worth taking, regardless of the amount of profit involved. A business purpose at its core is the answer to the question "What would I do if I had all the money I needed for the rest of my life?"

Another question can also reveal the implicit or explicit purpose of a business. When the business leader asks "How will the world be different tomorrow as a result of what we do today?", the answer reveals those changes that actually occur, whether the leader has intended them or not. Over time, as the question is asked and answered repeatedly, the purpose of the business becomes increasingly visible. The changes in the world that occur as a result of business operations form a mosaic of actions, which, when we step back to consider these actions over time, forms a pattern that reveals the purpose of the business.

As the entrepreneur considers their business purpose, they usually ask themselves a series of questions, these three being the most common:

- What need will this business's products and services fill?
- How will this business improve the lives of its customers?
- Is there a better way to meet a human need than what exists today?

By seeking answers to these questions, the business founder develops an idea of what will be important for the business to achieve – its purpose for existing. This purpose will enable the company to serve human needs in ways that are not currently being done by other existing products or services. The critical difference for building a long-lived company is to link from the business purpose to one or more specific human needs.

The core business purpose and its linkage to human needs form what is sometimes called the "founder's credo." What we observe in every long-lived company is that its purpose, usually stated in terms of a founder's credo, has been carefully nurtured, preserved, and ingrained throughout all aspects of the business throughout time. Although stated in different ways – sometimes it is a poem, sometimes it is a tapestry, sometimes a mission statement, or even sometimes a simple sentence – the credo is an organizational treasure that is respected and carried down through time.

A credo does not have to be long or complex, but it does need to be capable of being internalized by employees and becoming part of the brand definition and customer experience. Here is an example credo from the firearms manufacturer Beretta, which was founded in 1526:

> *Prudence and boldness.*
> *Quality without compromise.*

Here is a slightly longer example from Ritz-Carlton Hotels, which was founded in 1927:

> *The Ritz-Carlton Hotel is a place where the genuine care and comfort of our guests is our highest mission.*
> *We pledge to provide the finest personal service and facilities for our guests, who will always enjoy a warm, relaxed, yet refined ambience.*
> *The Ritz-Carlton experience enlivens the senses, instills wellbeing, and fulfills even the unexpressed wishes and needs of our guests.*

Here is a third example from Zildjian Cymbals, which was founded in 1623:

- *To expand the Company's global leadership as the "only serious choice" in cymbals, drumsticks and selected specialty percussion instruments by providing superior quality, product innovation, and outstanding customer service.*
- *To strive for continuous improvement through professional management and employee participation, while building the Company's value, preserving its family character, and enhancing its rich heritage.*

These examples provide clear values that can be translated directly into a brand image. Brand alignment is one of the core competencies of sustainable companies. Many long-term companies have succeeded in building on the owner's credo, mission, or purpose statement to create a set of carefully tended values and beliefs. It is these fundamental values and beliefs that are preserved and passed down through time to all employees and managers, and that form the basis for the business brand.

A clear business purpose establishes the reason for why the company is necessary in the world and what type of value it offers for all stakeholders, not just customers. A purpose offers a point of view for employees, helping them to understand how their efforts are directed towards making the world a better place. A clear purpose can transform employees into ambassadors, and customers into advocates: acting not because they have to, but because they want to. It is the stand the company managers and employees are making for what they believe is important in making society better off. Finally, a clear purpose is a source of inspiration to those within the company and those whose lives are touched by company actions. Companies with a clearly defined purpose, such as Patagonia and Royal Robbins, inspire their employees to go out and volunteer with an organization of their choosing, and provide paid time off for this activity. Employees are inspired to not only provide dedicated service to the company, but also assist other organizations with the same or similar purposes.

From a competitive advantage frame, customers buy the reason a company exists, not what the company does. Customers who purchase a company's products and services are obtaining artifacts and experiences that support their self-concept and social identity – they are resonating with the company's purpose. In effect, the customers are saying that part of who they are is reflected in the purpose of the company, and supporting the company makes them more of who they see themselves to be

An example of people purchasing products from a sustainability-based company is Patagonia. The company mission is "Build the best product, cause no unnecessary harm, and use business to inspire and implement solutions to the environmental crisis." The purpose of the company, however, is somewhat different and is stated succinctly here:

> Yet the depth and breadth of technological innovation of the past few decades shows that we have not lost our most useful gifts; humans are ingenious, adaptive, clever. We also have moral capacity, compassion for life, and an appetite for justice. We now need to more fully engage these gifts to make economic life more socially just and environmentally responsible, and less destructive to nature and the commons that sustain us.

People who purchase Patagonia products have a self-concept that includes cleverness and adaptability, compassion for life and a sense of fairness. Moreover, it is highly likely these individuals are committed to some form of social justice and environmental responsibility.

How a company goes about achieving its purpose can be defined as the set of methods and systems that it uses on a daily basis to augment its unique value proposition. In short, it is the activities that managers have chosen so that the company can perform in ways to support its purpose. These methods and systems can include customer service, continual improvement, employee knowledge and skill development, cost control systems, quality and environmental management, and community relations.

What a company does is best understood as a characterization of the activities in which it partakes – its specific industry. What every company does is to apply a specific type of technology in the production of its goods and services. In the language of economics, what a company does is to transform a specific set of inputs into a specific set of outputs by applying a distinctive combination of actions. Some examples of what companies do are manufacturing computers, growing and processing sugar from cane, or providing medical services.

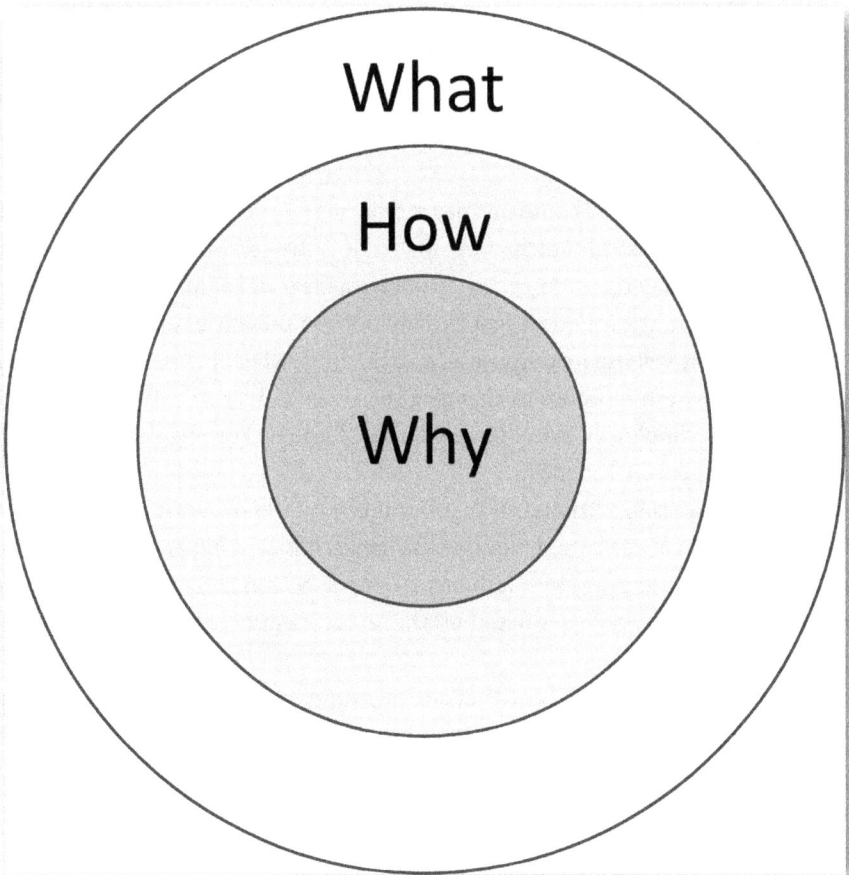

Figure 7. The role of business purpose.

Keiunkan's Purpose

The purpose of the Keiunkan Nishiyama Onsen is simple: to advance the wellbeing of people. How the company achieves this purpose is by providing an atmosphere of tranquility and harmony supported by outstanding service, restorative waters, cleanliness, and a strong connection to the natural world. What the company *does* is to operate a hot springs inn.

Putting It Together

When we integrate all three aspects of company activities together – why a company exists, how it achieves its purpose in the world, and what it does – we form the basis for leading with the Thousand Year Model. The combination of aspects is shown in Figure 21. It is the unique combination of purpose, methods, and products and services that forms both a competitive advantage and the foundation for a long lived business, and it is the leader's job to align this combination as the company and its operating environment evolve.

Over time, a long-lived company may modify what it does and how it does it, but its core purpose will remain unchanged. In fact, it is the central job of the leaders of a long-lived company to reinforce and maintain a clear definition of the company's core purpose. From the founder's first exclamations to present day operations, a sustainable company will use its purpose as an axis about which methods, systems, and products can pivot in response to changing social needs, market and fashion trends, and emerging technologies. We explore the role of leaders keeping the purpose alive more in the chapter on leadership.

The key to leading a Thousand Year Company is to know what can change and what must remain inviolate and immune to change. It is certainly true that technologies change over time along with fashions. A long-lived company will continually refine and adapt its technologies based on the latest scientific advances without ever losing sight of its purpose.

When Yuji took the reins at Keiunkan, he found a hotel that had not been improved for some time. He set about renovating the buildings, including new interiors, more rooms, more staff, and improved bathing facilities. He began working directly with local farmers and fishermen to purchase food grown locally and served fresh. He worked to improve the how and what of Keiunkan – creating an atmosphere of tranquility and harmony supported by outstanding service, restorative waters, cleanliness, and a strong connection to the natural world – while never losing sight of its main purpose. The development was not luxury for the sake of luxury, but luxury as part of an experience co-created with the natural world to promote people's wellbeing.

A long-lived company will change how it operates and may even change what it does, but it does not change its purpose. Its purpose remains central to what the company does, and how it finds its way in the world based on navigating a tumultuous operating environment. Leaders seek to adjust company operations to changing times and technologies, and look for new ways to fulfill the company's core purpose as the world goes forward.

Adaptation

In any ecosystem, the key to any living organism's survival is the capacity to adapt to changes in the greater environment without losing its life. These changes, known as perturbations, can come from weather pattern shifts, violent storms, volcanic eruptions, new competition for food, or mass extinctions due to disease. Ecosystems and organisms, such as human beings, that can adapt to significant changes are considered highly resilient. In biological terms, resilience is the amount of disturbance or perturbation that an ecosystem can withstand without changing self-organized processes and structures. Alternatively, resilience can be considered a measure of the amount of time a system takes to return to its prior state after being disturbed. Ecosystems evolve over time, within the constraints of the external environment and genetic potential of their constituent life forms, to the state most resilient to perturbation. This means that ecosystems tend towards dynamic homeostasis and stability, maximizing their ability to absorb and respond to shocks from the external environment.

When we apply the resilience concept to a human organization such as a company, we see that an organization's capacity to adapt to change is a critical factor in determining its longevity and sustainability, as well as its ability to support the economic needs of its owners. The greater the capacity to adapt to change, the more likely it is that the organization will survive and maintain its core structures and processes in the face of economic, social, ecological, and technological changes. According to the business advisors at the Prosci Group, the capacity to adapt to change requires that leaders take action in several arenas:

- *Preparing for change:* Defining the operating environment and preparing for possible changes in that environment.

- *Mitigating change*: Resisting and absorbing perturbations to reduce the consequences and impacts on the organization.
- *Responding to change*: Implementing tasks, activities, programs, and systems to adapt to the adverse effects of a change that cannot be resisted or absorbed.
- *Recovering from change*: Returning the organization to a prior stable state or to another stable state that is aligned with its core purpose.

The effect of leadership on adaptive capacity is critical in making sure that capacity is adequate to handle the most likely situations. However, some organizations reviewed for this book have survived the complete collapse of the societies in which they operated and have still remained viable business entities. This large capacity for adaptation is a hallmark of the strong leadership exercised within these organizations.

Adaptation Strategies
• Continual improvement of processes and systems
• Empowering and trusting employees to make the best choices
• Keep processes and systems simple and straightforward
• Socialize employees in the core values of the company
• Hold employees accountable for achieving long-term goals

Table 3. Adaptation Strategies

There are several ways in which the leaders in sustainable companies support organizational adaptation. The first way is by encouraging and modeling a kaizen approach, including rewarding and recognizing employee improvement achievements. The kaizen approach helps the company prepare for, mitigate, and respond to changes, and instills a sense of responsibility for adaptation in followers.

Kaizen is based on making small improvements in processes and systems on a continual basis, and includes changes resulting from new employee knowledge gained from both self-development efforts, as well as learning from stakeholder interactions. Kaizen helps the organization to (a) adapt to shifting stakeholder requirements, (b) optimize processes and systems for better performance, and (c) integrate new scientific knowledge into the technological capital that the company uses. These strategies ensure that the company makes many small adjustments to changing conditions as part of its business activities, and that employees view change as an opportunity for improvement rather than as a threat to the status quo.

The second way in which leaders in sustainable companies support organizational adaptation is by empowering and trusting employees to make the best choices available to them consonant with the business purpose. Because the leader reinforces the company values and credo through modeling as well as implements a compensation structure tied to the success of the organization as a whole, followers are trusted to make the choices that are in the best interests of the company. Leaders delegate significant decision-making authority to followers to make changes, which also supports a more effective kaizen approach. Leaders can let go of the need to be involved in all decisions because they align the company to desired goals using compensation that is tied to these goals.

Thirdly, leaders in sustainable companies focus on fighting process and system complexity. Sustainability leaders understand that there is a natural trend for systems and processes to become more complex over time, and they help their managers to break down complex systems into their essential elements and limit the degree of complexity those systems can attain. Moreover, sustainable company leaders understand that as systems and processes become more complex, not only are they more difficult and time-consuming to manage, but they are also less amenable to change – change and adaption become more difficult. Thus, the goal of complexity leadership is to keep systems and processes relatively simple while focusing them on the core business purpose, values, and credo.

However, this system balancing must be done carefully with the Law of Requisite Variety in mind. This law, according to William Buckley, editor of the book *Modern Systems Research for the Behavioral Scientist,* states that "the variety within a system must be at least as great as the environmental variety against which it is attempting to regulate itself." A simple example is a thermostat for a heater. The thermostat has a wide range of temperature settings, while the heater simply turns on and off. In a business, requisite variety means that company leaders encourage the participation of a diverse population as well as implement changes to many different systems and processes that might be affected by a single change to the operating environment.

For example, if a supplier that has been with the company suddenly goes out of business, the leader first needs to gather all of the individuals who are affected by the products and services that the supplier provided and make an informed assessment of the impact of the loss of that supplier. Such an assessment will include the informed decisions of those throughout the company who, having been thoroughly socialized in its core values, will define choices that promote the best interests of both the company and its employees. Then the leader, taking a holistic view of the company, might make changes to production, finance and accounting, legal, information technology, and planning systems. However, if these systems are very complex, and as a result, the changes take a long time to make, the company might not be able to continue operating until it has found an acceptable replacement supplier and integrated the new supplier into company processes. If too much time is needed to make the necessary changes across the organization, the company risks going out of business.

Therefore, the leader should strive to build a certain degree of complexity into the company based on reasonably foreseeable events, but no more than what is needed – the proliferation of complexity stops based on reasonable predictability. The leader should select the stakeholder relationships to be pursued and the structure of operating systems and processes based on the likelihood that changes in stakeholder status will necessitate a change in the operational realities of the company.

Fourthly, through overseeing and imbuing the company's socialization processes with core values, leaders in sustainable companies make sure that newly hired employees are properly trained and motivated. The goal is for all employees to internalize the core values of the company. When employees are confronted with an obstacle or change-inducing force, they can be trusted to make the extra effort to overcome any problem and avoid serious disruption of operations. Sustainability leaders, by serving as models of the core values and credo, help their followers to remain centered on what is important and reinforce the employee's importance to the success of the company.

Finally, leaders in sustainable companies hold their followers accountable for achieving important goals related to sustainable operations. This sense of accountability anchors follower actions in reality, and grounds the entire company. When they know they are both trusted and accountable for achieving meaningful objectives, people will assume responsibility for their achievement without question. Followers will commit to taking action because they understand that the actions will benefit the organization and help drive it towards a future outcome that is both significant and meaningful: survival and flourishing.

One of the best examples of adaptation is the Van Eegehn company, which was founded in 1662 by Jacob van Eeghen as a sea-based trading company, shipping wool, wine, salt and sugar from the Baltic Sea to the West Indies. Over the years since its founding, the company has continually adapted to changes in its operating environment by expanding or contracting its shipping and trading operations numerous times, and at one point it owned a bank and several other trading companies that have subsequently been sold. Throughout all of the changes, the leaders have made sure that the company has retained its basic focus on trading foodstuffs and related products, and has approached its customers with respect, honesty, and transparency. Today the company has evolved into a leading international distributor of specialty nutraceuticals and functional ingredients.

Maintaining such a focus on trading has required the ability to understand customer needs and market requirements, and to find the best suppliers that can meet these needs. The core values of the company include continuity, reliability, flexibility and providing an extremely high level of personalized service. Such core values have influenced the business operations and strategic decisions over the last four centuries. While maintaining its status as a trading company and growing deep expertise in sourcing, product development, marketing, and supply chain management, the company has approached the global operating environment flexibly, shifting the traded products and services to meet the changing needs of the modern world. At the company's beginning, it specialized in food ingredients such as spices, coffee, and cacao, while today it has shifted its trading to natural and synthetic vitamins, botanical extracts, and antioxidants.

Adaptability in companies is set through the core values as modeled by the leaders and expressed in their behaviors. Through modeling the credo and values and providing extensive training and socialization designed to help employees internalize the company's core values, leaders provide a center to which the organization returns after experiencing a disturbance. Aligning the different elements of the organization in response to a disturbance, leaders seek to return the company to a stable state that fulfills its business purpose. Thus the roles of leaders are to help the company prepare for change through learning-based stakeholder relationships, supporting continual improvement and systems simplicity to absorb disturbances, empowering and motivating followers so they take actions to respond to changes, and steering the organization to stable states after disruptions.

Keiunkan's Adaptation Strategies

For Keiunkan, adaptation is an essential element of leadership and requires constant attention. The physical environment in which the ryokan operates is highly geologically active with frequent floods, landslides, and road washouts. Yuji is constantly aware of the state of the environment, including transportation, and makes changes as necessary. For example, in the autumn of 2013 when the road was partially washed out due to a heavy rain, he hired a van to transport customers from the town of Hayakawa to the inn so they would not have to negotiate the hazardous driving conditions, and lowered the price of the rooms and meals temporarily to keep a full occupancy. Several years ago when a landslide destroyed part of the building, he contracted with a local company to rebuild it in a more modern style. This is an example of Keiunkan's strategies for adapting to change, detailed below:

- *Preparing for change:* Yuji is in constant communication with local community and government leaders as well as construction companies.
- *Mitigating change:* The current building is constructed of reinforced concrete with a wood interior, which is highly resistant to the type of damages that occurred during the last landslide. Yuji worked with local governments and contractors to improve the road to the inn so that it will be less likely to be damaged in the future.
- *Responding to change:* When the road was washed out due to flooding, Yuji made sure that the van was operating constantly to keep the flow of guests moving throughout the day and night.
- *Recovering from change:* Yuji modifies the pricing structure constantly to account for changing occupancy rates due to seasonality, weather events, and holidays. This approach to flexible pricing has kept the occupancy rate at a year-round average of 80% while maintaining an atmosphere of quiet and relaxation.

An important part of adapting to change is finding the energy to keep up the continual improvement effort. Leaders play an important role here: long-term follower motivation is a central item on their agendas. The energy required to keep a company stable and functioning during periods of significant change can be considerable, and leaders need to make sure that their followers are motivated to sustain their adaptation efforts.

Energy

One of the more noticeable characteristics of a sustainable company is a sense of passion and commitment to getting the job done. This sense of passion is a primary source of employee motivation to perform well. Leaders in the sustainable company have a special responsibility: to continually refresh and reinforce the relevant sources of motivation that support follower behaviors directed towards the survival of the company, and to make sure that each employee has a desire for and a strong commitment to doing the job well. Leaders have to understand the salient forms of motivation for all employees, and interact with them to deepen and extend the factors that influence their energy levels. While there are literally dozens of sources of individual motivation within organizations, only the five that are highly relevant for sustainable organizations are discussed here: social learning, human needs, meaningfulness, biophilia, and tradition.

One of the first and most readily apparent sources of human motivation stems from social learning. People tend to imitate those with whom they are in regular contact, especially when those being modeled are observed to be successful and are rewarded for specific behaviors. Leaders, whether they intend to or not, are constantly being observed by employees as models and as sources of directed behaviors to be emulated. These directed behaviors, when made apparent through widespread contact and communication, form the basis for observational learning on the part of followers. Followers internalize expectations about what behaviors are desirable, and thus imitate the behaviors of leaders.

The implications of social learning-based motivation are important. First, leaders must hold themselves to a higher standard than employees, as they are being observed during all activities in which they are visible to employees. This means being very careful about messages communicated and actions taken. Second, leaders must act in ways consistent with the credo and core values. This means that every leader must have internalized the credo and values completely, and act unthinkingly in ways that align with the credo and core values. For decisions that require more extended deliberations, leaders need to make it clear to followers how they are applying the credo and core values to determine an appropriate course of action. This is particularly critical during times of change in which employees might have differing opinions on what the direction the company should go. In the end, the average employee doesn't need to feel that their opinion is the best one: what they need to feel is that their opinion has been considered and that a competent pilot is flying the plane.

Another important implication of social learning is that the leader is presenting an image of a *possible self* to employees. This possible self can reinforce the employee's confidence that they can attain the goals of the company, and gives employees an idea of what type of person they could become as a result of being a member of the organization. Modeling a possible self also shows employees the paths to achieving important goals as well as the behaviors that will take them along these paths. Being in the presence of a possible self that is contributing to the organization's success opens employees up to the emotions of hope and excitement at becoming a similarly significant person.

A second source of motivation is human needs fulfillment. Leader actions can help employees by opening pathways within the organization through which both their needs and the company's needs are fulfilled. According to need theory, people are motivated by needs to exhibit behaviors to meet those needs on a continual basis. We strive to meet our needs to both avoid problems and to grow and become better.

There is an important needs-related group dynamic that leaders of sustainable companies must address. This dynamic is the tendency of a group, as it achieves its common goals and gains resources, to begin to focus on the individual needs of the group members rather than on the needs of the group as a whole. The members will tend to emphasize the differences between themselves and the other group members, and increasing attention is paid to personal needs and the importance of the group needs is diminished. This shift results in decreased functioning and eventual group disintegration.

The leaders of sustainable companies must address this dynamic head on. In the Thousand Year Model, leaders take specific actions to meet both individual and organizational needs simultaneously. These actions are shown in Table 9. An important point to remember for needs-based motivation is that leaders strive continually to help followers understand that there is a direct convergence between the organization's needs and each person's needs, and as members of the company they can best meet their own needs by helping the company to meet its needs. As such, leaders in a sustainable company constantly reinforce the intersection of company needs and personal needs, and orchestrate the fulfillment of both.

Need	Leader Actions to Fulfill Individual Needs	Leader Actions to Fulfill Organizational Needs
Subsistence	Reinforcement of the idea of the company as a means of survival – food, shelter, and work – for all	Reinforcement of the idea of the necessity for the company to survive for the long term, reinforcement of the provision of only singular or synergistic satisfiers
Protection	Reinforcement of the idea of being part of something special, provision of meaningful employment, support for cooperation to achieve important goals	Reinforcement of the provision of only singular or synergistic satisfiers, creation of a strong culture

Affection	Creation of an atmosphere of respect and tolerance, fostering receptivity to new ideas, supporting employee passion for the work	Creation of strong stakeholder relationships and partnerships
Understanding	Emphasis on learning, mastery, and continual improvement	Emphasis on learning from stakeholder relationships
Participation	Supporting a high degree of employee involvement and empowerment, creation of a strong sense of affiliation with the company	Managing conflict for optimal outcomes
Idleness	Creation of peace of mind based on a commitment to a stable company	Support for reasonable work hours and adequate free time, both on and off the job
Creation	Supporting employee imagination, inventiveness, and curiosity	Strong commitment to experimenting with new technologies, processes, and systems
Identity	Creation of a strong sense of belongingness, differentiation, status, and special group membership unique club	Internalization of credo and core values, modeling of behavioral norms, reinforcement of distinct brand identity
Freedom	Support for employee empowerment, self-determination, open-mindedness	Continual improvement and problem-solving

Table 4. Leader Actions to Support Need-Based Motivation

A third source of motivation that sustainability leaders consider is meaningfulness and a sense of purpose. People can experience a sense of meaningfulness when they can observe that their work connects to a purpose that is important to them, and that has value for those individuals with whom they share significant relationships. Leaders have a special responsibility to connect the dots here, and help people to realize that their jobs are about much more than simply making money. They should establish for employees the impacts of employee actions on other people and on the natural world, which provides a context for responsibility. The goal is to strengthen employees' perceptions that their actions have a positive impact on both stakeholders and on the organization itself.

One of the central aspects of meaningfulness is doing well: the actions that one takes are meaningful because they have positive impacts on stakeholders, both now and in the future. These impacts are a direct result of the company enacting fully what it stands for in the world, and by doing so achieving its purpose. Rather than a singular focus on extrinsic rewards such as money and material wealth, leaders of sustainable companies emphasize a sense of intrinsic motivation based on the personal satisfaction employees obtain from fulfilling a meaningful purpose and contributing to the greater good of the company and of the world at large.

An important consideration when working with meaningfulness is the idea of balance. Leaders must maintain a rather delicate balance when promulgating purpose-based goals. Employees are motivated by more than just meaningfulness: they are motivated by *hedonic goals* such as having fun, enjoying their work, and feeling excited about what they do every day, as well as *gain-based goals* that include opportunities to increase rewards, both monetary and non-monetary. The job of sustainability leaders is to help employees understand the high priority of the organization's purpose, and that the company must achieve its purpose effectively before employees can realize either hedonic or gain-based goals.

Purpose comes first, and a well-led company will enable employees to realize the importance of purpose by reinforcing it with rewards linked to the overall functioning of the organization, communicating symbols of core values, and publicly celebrating employees whose achievements reflect exemplary fulfillment of the company purpose. Leaders must demonstrate how achieving the company's purpose also makes economic and ecological sense, both now and in the longer term. Leaders must not allow short-term pressures for economic gain to overshadow the primary importance of achieving the purpose, and must show employees how profits are the result of doing good things. The message is that the company will be successful when it brings value to its stakeholders, and this success will be translated into profits when its operations are efficient.

One way to approach the integration of purpose is to apply the *and* approach, as exemplified by Daniel Lubetzky, the CEO of the KIND company. The core of this approach is that it rejects the false tradeoff between profit, social responsibility, and environmental integrity, and asserts that it is possible to obtain all three simultaneously. Rather than having to choose between profit or social responsibility, or choose between profit or environmental integrity, the *and* approach posits that a company can obtain profit *and* social responsibility *and* environmental integrity concurrently.

The KIND Company is a manufacturer of snacks. Daniel has imbued the company with a clear mission: "Do the KIND thing for your body, your taste buds, and the world." Such a mission contains an implicit dual sense of purpose: to create good tasting, healthy food that fights diabetes and obesity, and to use the profits from the sales of these snacks to promote positive social change. What becomes important is balance between product quality and social action. The products must taste good, contain ingredients that promote personal health through good nutrition, and be loved by customers. The customer demand will in turn will drive sufficient revenues to allow for meaningful social actions to take place. KIND's social actions have included connecting troops with their loved ones, providing the less fortunate with life essentials, and empowering young adults with cancer. Although the company has existed only since 2004, this **and** approach to a balanced purpose is shared by many of the long-lived companies.

A second consideration when working with meaningfulness is the alignment of systems that support achieving the organization's purpose, and the balance of meaningfulness with both hedonic and gain-based goals. In practice, this means that aligning employee compensation, community and other stakeholder interactions, governance, and employee learning to the central purpose of the company. In addition, sustainability leaders must make sure that these systems are optimized in terms of how they interact with each other. For example, learning from stakeholders is a waste of time unless the ideas gained are translated into strategy changes, new product developments, or operational improvements.

A fourth and perhaps more subtle source of motivation with which sustainability leaders should be concerned stems from the idea of biophilia, which E. O. Wilson has defined as "the love of life" or "humans' innate tendency to focus on living things, as opposed to the inanimate." Wilson describes biophilia as "humans' innate affinity for other living things born out of our evolution among creatures and habitats of nature over countless centuries." Biophilia can also be defined more generally as the love of nature. In our increasingly artificial work environments, it is easy for leaders to overlook this understated yet powerful source of human motivation.

It is easy to see biophilia in action. Simply place a puppy with a child and watch what happens. In adults, the biophilic effect is noticeable, for example among those who spend time in the wilds or who spend time and effort on environmental concerns. In architectural design, a new breed of buildings is emerging where, according to the Yale School of Forestry and Environmental Studies, we are designing "buildings that connect people and nature – hospitals where patients heal faster, schools where children's test scores are higher, offices where workers are more productive, and communities where people know more of their neighbors and families thrive."

Through a continuing barrage of newscasts, newspaper and magazine articles, and first person experiences, the world's population has become widely aware of the negative effects of humans on the Earth's ecosystems. These effects are destroying the biosphere, the thin membrane of life that surrounds the Earth and supports all forms of life, including human life. The impacts on our psyches are a direct assault on our biophilic instincts.

Rather than a contempt for other non-human forms of life that support us, leaders in sustainable companies foster a sense of responsibility and stewardship for the natural world. Rather than objectify the natural world as a set of resources for humans to exploit, sustainable company leaders foster a sense of interrelatedness with the ecosystems that provide life support and other services upon which the company depends for its existence. In a company that supports and nurtures a biophilic perspective, negative impacts such as toxic pollution are simply not tolerated, as they are viewed as an attack on oneself. The wise sustainability leader understands that the motivating power of biophilia, and reinforces their organization's alignment with the natural world while making this alignment part of day-to-day life. The point is to ground the organization's operations in nature, which will support the power of biophilia to drive employees' actions and decisions.

A final source of motivation derives from leaders acting to constantly refresh the organizational memory, defining and upholding the traditions on which the company is based. It is easy for employees to forget why the company was founded in the first place as well as its significant accomplishments over time. These two ideas must form the basis for an ongoing dialog with employees. Leaders can reinforce the core ideas which led the founders to start the company, describe the significant events in its history, and instill a sense of pride and personal ownership at being part of the continuing enterprise. Additionally, the credo reinforcement can serve as a means to embed decision criteria into the company: when everyone knows what the right thing to do is, there is much less need for executive management involvement in day-to-day decisions as well as greater trust that the right choices will be made on an ongoing basis.

Energy at Keiunkan

Yuji Fukazawa has a commanding presence. When he walks through the inn, employees immediately show respect through their tone of voice, body language, and by bowing. They listen attentively when he speaks. His personal assistant is ever at the ready to support him, hovering nearby when not directly engaged in management activities. It is clear that Yuji is the keeper of the tradition: his knowledge and decision making authority are accepted unquestioningly.

The energy level among the employees is subdued, relaxed yet highly attentive with a powerful undercurrent of strength. When one enters the inn, one steps into a place where time runs more slowly, where the ghosts of the past are as alive as the guests of today. There is an air of quiet professionalism among all of the staff, which Yuji reinforces through training and meetings. One gets the sense of a powerful, slow moving train that moves unceasingly towards its destination.

It is in the selection of the staff where Yuji most shows his strength as a leader. Yuji seeks people who have an affinity for the mountains, a love of nature, a knowledge of and a desire to carry on the tradition of the onsen, business experience, and polite manners. He selects these from the local community, including visitors to local families. He also seeks out people who vacation in the area, as they are more likely to appreciate the beauty and quiet of the rural setting of the inn. He does admit that it is difficult to find the right type of person, but he will not compromise on his selections, as he knows that people who share the same values and beliefs will be better employees, and will be motivated to perform well in all instances.

This tenacity and particularity pay off in the level of service the guests can expect. Yuji knows that by finding people who possess the intrinsic motivation to serve and revitalize the guests, he will create a staff that possesses the energy to create an exceptional guest experience. By fanning the flames of this motivation through high compensation, fair policies, and a sense of pride in supporting a tradition stretching back generations, Yuji can focus on strategic issues and trust that each person will do their utmost to uphold the tradition of the inn and take care of the daily operations.

Time

One of the most salient and distinguishing characteristics of sustainability leaders is how they approach time. Within a sustainable organization, leaders reinforce the perception of time as the organization's most precious resource, the resource upon which all other resources depend. Time is seen as more valuable than money, new ideas, individual relationships, or even ecosystem services. Leaders recognize that nothing the company does will give it more time, and nothing the company does will allow the company to regain time that was misspent on spurious or even damaging activities. Leaders know that there simply cannot be more than twenty-four hours in a day no matter what happens, so it is the way the company takes advantage of those hours that matters most.

The first important implication from the recognition that time is the sustainable organization's most precious resource is this: the ways in which employees spend their time is the foundation of the organization's success. Thus, we see the importance of aligning employee efforts to human needs, guiding and moderating changes, and setting performance standards. The quality of the organization's efforts through time are the essence of its success.

An especially significant part of any leader's job in a sustainable company is expanding the time awareness surrounding how the company meets human needs. This expanded awareness is essential if the company is to make sure that satisfying one need does not result in the destruction of another need, the company is meeting human needs in the most effective way possible, and that short-term solutions do not result in excessive long-term costs that exceed the benefits of the solution. This discernment is essential to decisions that support the pursuit of different technology options as well as different business models, as what appears to be a reasonable short-term solution may in fact result in long-term social, ecological, and economic costs that render the solution meaningless or even detrimental.

For example, nuclear power in the short term meets the need of subsistence through generating the electricity we use in our daily lives and business operations. However, when we take a life cycle view of this form of power, we can achieve a different perspective. We see that this form of power generation creates large amounts of toxic waste that cannot be disposed of safely using current technologies; therefore, nuclear power in the long term generates costs in excess of the benefits that the short-term power generation provides. Another example is coal-based electric power. While coal-based electricity supports subsistence in the short term, in the longer term, the greenhouse gases that this form of power generation creates threaten all life on Earth with extinction. Thus, we see that coal-fired power plants in the short term support subsistence, but in the longer term they are actually destroyers of subsistence.

A key time-based task for leaders in a sustainable company is to keep employees focused on the organization's driving forces, such as building stakeholder relationships, gaining mastery, and learning to improve. Indeed, it is these driving forces that develop the quality of employees' time so they can function more effectively in the present. Since time is flowing constantly, what employees do in the present is both forming the organization's past as well as setting the direction for its future. Thus, the key to creating a desired trajectory through time is to function more effectively in the present by creating a positively-perceived past and moving towards a desirable and meaningful future.

Functioning effectively in the present requires an awareness of the different time scales with which humans are connected. Freeman Dyson, on page 341 of his book *From Eros to Gaia*, has described these time scales nicely:

The destiny of our species is shaped by the imperatives of survival on six distinct time scales. To survive means to compete successfully on all six time scales. But the unit of survival is different at each of the six time scales. On a time scale of years, the unit is the individual. On a time scale of decades, the unit is the family. On a time scale of centuries, the unit is the tribe or nation. On a time scale of millennia, the unit is the culture. On a time scale of tens of millennia, the unit is the species. On a time scale of eons, the unit is the whole web of life on our planet. Every human being is the product of adaptation to the demands of all six time scales. That is why conflicting loyalties are deep in our nature. In order to survive, we have needed to be loyal to ourselves, to our families, to our tribes, to our cultures, to our species, to our planet. If our psychological impulses are complicated, it is because they were shaped by complicated and conflicting demands.

Leaders in sustainable companies can use the Thousand Year Model to address each of these complicated and conflicting demands and link to each of the different time scales. In fact, it is by aligning the elements of the model in their organization that the leaders can address the needs of the different durations needed for change. Stewart Brand, in his book *The Clock of the Long Now*, has refined Dyson's framework to link the periods of change with specific areas of human endeavor. In Table 5, both Dyson's and Brand's frameworks are refined even further and include representative decisions made for changes that occur within each of the different time periods noted.

Time scale	The Rate of Change	Unit of Analysis	Representative Decisions	Knowledge Areas
Years	≈ 1	Individual	• What kind of car (clothes, food, equipment, experience, etc.) should I buy? • What kind of job do I want to do?	Fashion and values
Decades	≈ 10	Organization	• How should we structure our organization? • What does organizational effectiveness mean? • How should our organization participate in markets?	Economics and commerce
Centuries	≈ 100	Tribe/Nation	• What kind of infrastructure (buildings, roads, water systems, communication systems, educational systems, etc.) should we build to support our society? • How should we organize our society to meet the needs of our people? • Who should rule?	Politics and governance

Millennia	≈ 1000	Human culture	• What ideas, values, beliefs, and behaviors best support our continued existence? • What symbols, interpretations, and perspectives give our lives meaning?	Philosophy, psychology, theology, sociology, anthropology, and linguistics
Tens of Millennia	≈ 10,000	Species	• How can we keep habitats and landscapes thriving? • How can we support biodiversity? • How can humans best adapt to the Earth's living environment?	Flora and fauna, evolutionary biology, sociobiology
Ages	≈ 1,000,000	Earth's geological and ecological systems	• How can we avoid increasing concentrations of either (a) substances extracted from the Earth's crust, or (b) substances produced by society? • How can we avoid physical degradation of the Earth's living systems?	Nature, ecology, geology

Table 5. The Time Considerations of Sustainable Organizations

There are three important points to remember about the different time periods associated with human civilization in the world and the sustainable company. The first point is that a sustainable company will ideally locate itself within a 1000-year time frame, and thus align its purpose within cultural perspectives. Such a purpose does not lend itself to change over the shorter period, and indeed even ensures that the company might remain relevant for a thousand years. Such a company can endure changes at the national, organizational, and individual level while remaining centered on its core values and purpose, which change at a much slower pace because they are linked to core cultural values and beliefs.

The second point is that the different tempos of change mean that leaders in a sustainable company can easily connect their decisions to impacts likely to occur in the shorter realms, and adjust their organizations to feedback at quicker paces. These decisions require a time-awareness of the impacts from each decision as well as an awareness of which time realm subsumes the factors that are likely to affect these decisions. For example, it would be easy to receive feedback from decisions made in the realm of fashion within a year or sometimes even a few months. The lesson is that leaders who operate in a longer time frame can still make decisions affecting shorter time frames relatively easily because changes within these time frames are visible to them.

The third and perhaps most salient point is that it is difficult for leaders of sustainable organizations to appreciate the longer-term changes taking place at the species and Earth's geological and ecological systems levels. Because of our limited human lifetime and attention span, the best that leaders can do is to approximate the likely impacts that these decisions will have on these slower-paced, longer-term realms. Many of the most important changes in the life support systems of the Earth may be so gradual as to be imperceptible to our limited human cognitive abilities. Gradual deterioration of the Earth's living systems due to the negative impacts of human civilizations may not be noticeable until it is too late to reverse the impacts of the changes. Therefore, in recognition of the difficulty of assessing such long-term impacts, sustainability leaders will take a precautionary approach for decisions that might impact the continued viability of the Earth's living systems.

Bristol-Myers Squibb, which was founded in 1858, illustrates how to address these three points. As part of its corporate governance, the company follows a set of clearly defined values, principles, and ethical standards of conduct to support their conviction that "the priceless ingredient of every product is the honor and integrity of its maker." Part of this commitment is realized in the company's implementation of the Precautionary Principle: taking preventive action in the face of uncertainty to prevent harm. The leaders apply the principle to environmental protection, public health, and economic gain. The company practices supporting both its multiple time period awareness and precautionary approach include the following:

- Implementing an integrated environment, health and safety management system
- Managing risks as part of performance assessment, strategic planning, brand planning, performance management, disclosure, and crisis management
- Establishing a set of overarching policies that drive performance for simultaneous economic progress, social responsibility, and environmental protection
- Setting ten-year goals as a core part of its planning processes

An important consequence of acknowledging the different time perspectives in Table 11, and especially of the time perspective in which a sustainable company is located, is that the tempo of operations will be a function of the locus of change. At a sustainable company, the overall tempo of operations will be slower and less frenetic than at an unsustainable company. This slower tempo is due to the anchoring of major decision processes in multiple time periods. In other words, while the pace of material throughput may be high, the rate at which major changes are made is slow and thus imbues employees with a more relaxed and patient approach to business operations.

Sustainability leaders also focus their efforts on balancing change with continuity. They understand that although change can be exciting, too much change can produce anxiety and fear. Too much change can actually be counterproductive to achieving the goals of the company, while too little change can result in stagnation and eventual demise. The art of sustainability leadership is finding just the right amount of change to keep the company moving forward while avoiding both apprehension and boredom. Keeping traditions alive while adapting them to current times is one of the pillars of a sustainability leader's time-related efforts.

The leaders of sustainable companies do not allow their companies to become hide-bound and completely restrained by tradition, however. Leaders work to inculcate a balanced awareness of the past, present, and future for their companies. We might summarize the normative approach as follows:

- Gratitude for the past,
- Service for the present, and
- Responsibility for the future.

This normative approach is especially suitable in a number of different ways for leading a sustainable company. A positive, thankful attitude towards the past helps employees to experience appreciation and deep respect for the company traditions, as well as reframe any misfortunes or downturns that the company may have gone through. Rather than obsessing about the negative events in the past, a leader's affirmative attitude and active reframing helps employees realize how these events contributed to eventual positive outcomes. In a way, the leader becomes a living reminder of the past, modeling the values upon which the business was built.

In addition, such an attitude of gratitude fosters an appreciation for society-wide cultural traditions as well as national cultural variables that might directly influence business operations. Viewing past events in a positive light frees both leaders and followers to envision an even better future instead of being stuck in ruminating about things that did not go as planned.

Developing gratitude for the past is supported by the construction of memories, a psychological process in which people actively construct a version of what happened in the past based on their attitude towards the event. According to Zimbardo and Boyd, rather than recording data like a video camera, the human brain actively reconstructs memories based on current attitudes, beliefs, and available information. This active reconstruction process means that people's current moods and thoughts influence how they remember what happened in the past, whether or not the events actually took place. There is an important implication here: we cannot change the events that happened to us in the past, but we can change our attitudes towards and even our recollection of these events. Sustainability leaders can influence their followers to gain a positive attitude about past events, which will carry over to the present moment. When employees are freed from recriminations and regret for past actions, and leaders reinforce the positive impacts of those actions as well as link them to the core values of the company, employees can solve problems more effectively in the present.

A note of caution is needed here. Leaders should refrain from cheerleading, which can be seen as disingenuous. While reframing the past in a positive light is important, it is equally as important to be honest about company events, both historical and current. Rather than inculcating a slavish dedication to the ideals and values of the founder, sustainability leaders should respect the maturity of their followers by sharing important achievements, telling meaningful stories, and then allowing followers to internalize the core values of the company in their own way. Such respect is supported by transparency about company operations including important objectives. The message should be clear:

- This is where we have come from
- This is who we are as a company today
- As a valued employee your contributions are essential to help us sustain our operations

When leaders focus on service for the present, they can place emphasis on the links to organizational culture and the true satisfaction of human needs. This emphasis sets the agenda around which sustainability leaders can generate energy for the service-based mission of the company, which can then be expanded to create a compelling vision for the future. The goal is to help all members of the organization to function effectively in the present moment, which means going beyond an awareness of events in the very recent past and those likely to happen in the very near future. Leaders, by serving as the organizational memory, help followers to become aware of the influence of long past events as well as the likely impacts on future outcomes that might take decades to materialize, thus providing linkages to the different time considerations.

Another aspect of service for the present is the expansion of service to include decision factors that affect the different time considerations shown in Table 11. Service for the present in a sustainable company means more than just meeting human needs in the short term – it means meeting the needs of the different elements of change in the longer term as well. Service for the present means considering the impacts of a decision over all of the multiple time periods we have noted, and including the interests of those in each time period as part of the decision. In this way, service for the present becomes linked to positive future outcomes.

A company that directly addresses time frames, positive future outcomes, and service for the present is Seventh Generation, a manufacturer of dishwashing soap, laundry detergent, household cleaners, paper products, and personal care items. The company frames its goals in terms of four aspirations:

- We care today for the next seven generations of tomorrows
- We champion honesty, responsibility, and radical transparency in commerce
- We enhance health through education, activism, and innovation
- We advance social justice and equality to unleash human potential

According to its website, the company has set in place a five-year plan. This plan was based on an examination of the environmental, social, and economic impacts of the company and includes ways to adhere to the following principles: "responsible sourcing; using materials from plants not petroleum; ensuring the health of our planet and the people on it; having an engaged, motivated workforce; and caring for our community." Seventh Generation, by establishing these commitments, has agreed to take actions that will achieve results years, decades, and even centuries from now, all of which are centered on a strong sense of service for both people and the Earth. Although the company has been in existence only since 1990, its core values and aspirations center it firmly in the realm of sustainable operations.

A linkage to positive future outcomes becomes the foundation of responsibility for the future. Being responsible means acknowledging that a person is the cause for the outcomes of their decisions, and are being accountable for the results that may unfold over different periods of time in the future. The Iroquois Constitution summarizes this approach nicely: "Look and listen for the welfare of the whole people and have always in view not only the present but also the coming generations, even those whose faces are yet beneath the surface of the ground – the unborn of the future Nation."

The Iroquois Constitution also takes note of the fact that highly future-oriented decisions may be difficult, and the sustainability leader will encounter significant resistance from those individuals who desire more immediate rewards in the present. It goes on to provide this advice for leaders: "The thickness of your skin shall be seven spans – which is to say that you shall be proof against anger, offensive actions and criticism." This is an important point: linking sustainability decision outcomes to future events may cause negative impacts in the present, while the rewards associated with those outcomes may be delayed far into the future. This delay is the reason the publicly held corporation form of business is unsuited for sustainability management. Corporations require their managers to deliver quarterly economic returns which, in a sustainability management context, would in many cases have to be sacrificed for investments in a better future for the company. Managers who chose to make those significant sacrifices would quickly find themselves ousted from their organizations.

Another example of future-based responsibility can be found in the annals of Marco Polo, where he describes a visit to the town of Tingui in 1265 AD.

And again I tell you that the most beautiful vessels and plates of porcelain, large and small, that one could describe are made in great quantity in this aforesaid province in a city which is called Tingui, more beautiful than can be found in any other city. And on all sides they are very much valued, for none of them are made in another place but in this city, and from there they are carried to many places throughout the world. And there is plenty there and a great sale, so great that for one Venetian groat you would actually have three bowls so beautiful that none would know how to devise them better. And these bowls are made in this way, as he was told, of this kind of earth; namely, that those of the city gather as from a mine mud and rotten earth and make great mounds of it, and leave them thus in the wind, in the rain, and in the sun for thirty and forty years that they do not move the mounds. And then in this space of time the said earth being so long time in these mounds is so worked up that the bowls made of it have the color of azure, and they are very shining and most beautiful beyond measure. And you must know that when a man gathers that earth he gathers it for his sons or grandsons. It is clear that owing to the long time that it must lie quiet for its working up he does not hope to gain profit from it or put it into use, but the son who will survive him will reap the fruit of it.

Marco Polo: The Description of the World, translated and edited by A.C. Moule and Paul Pelliot, 1938, George Routledge & Sons Limited, London, England, p.352

In short, leaders of sustainable companies foster a sense of time beyond the recent past and near future, honoring traditions while creating a sense of hopefulness about the company and its path in the world. Anchored in the essence of human culture, leaders help their companies to make decisions that affect multiple time periods, and that can result in outcomes that the leaders may never personally experience for themselves. Honoring the past and treating traditions with respect, linking present day actions to human needs and transcendental ideals, and considering the impacts of decisions made today far into the future are all important tasks for the sustainability leader.

Time at Keiunkan

A different pace is immediately evident when one enters the Nishiyama Keiunkan Onsen. While the service is quick and efficient, the firm, which is more than a thousand years old, operates in a subdued manner using well-honed processes. No one is in a hurry, some of the surroundings have gone unchanged for centuries, and the atmosphere is one of relaxed professionalism. Such an operating tempo is affected directly by the organization's links with its past, which tend to slow the pace down as the company operates within the context of its traditions. The employees of the company exhibit patience and tolerance since they know that the leaders are dedicated to the survival and continuity of the business, and that there will be time to make the important decisions.

Yuji has made several significant efforts to balance tradition and innovation. Although employees are proud of and imbued with the tradition of the inn and its founding, they are open minded enough to consider new possibilities in improving the service for guests. Continual improvement is part of the credo. Yuji is "always looking to be better" in all aspects of the inn's operations, and influences his employees to adopt the kaizen approach. This approach is based on all employees making numerous small changes continually to improve both the quality of results and the efficiency of processes. Such small changes are evident in the recent remodeling efforts for the rooms and tubs, which have been restored to a traditional Japanese style while being fitted to maximize the guests' comfort.

Yuji's daily actions reflect a full consciousness of leading from the past, for the present, and towards the future. He has surrounded the employees with reminders of time including such things as the large shimekazari in the lobby, which is a sculpture decorated with auspicious items that symbolize desired present and future states of being as well as offer protection from bad spirits. Reminders of the inn's history are the traditional Japanese décor in the rooms and the original rock gardens. Underneath these artifacts are the latest in hotel and restaurant technologies, designed to provide guests with a luxurious and revitalizing experience. For the future, Yuji and his employees are planting trees, protecting the mountain environment through habitat restoration and by limiting development, and protecting the clean, pure water by building the best plumbing system available. It is through these actions that Yuji accepts and guides others through changes at the inn, and shows gratitude for the past, service for the present, and responsibility for the future.

Aesthetics

The word aesthetics is derived from the ancient Greek word *aisthesis* which means "of or pertaining to the perception of the senses." Aesthetics today is still firmly grounded in sense perception. The usage of the word has expanded considerably, and in today's leadership context we can conceive of aesthetics as having two important meanings:

- A style or a sensibility, which is further defined as a "perceptually cohesive organization of qualities – visual, auditory, gustatory, kinesthetic, and olfactory – that is distinct from other perceptually cohesive organizations of qualities." These organizations of forms are characterized by a whole indivisible into its component parts, as the parts simply do not express the same meaning until they are placed together according to a defined set of criteria such as contrast, balance, and harmony, or a widely accepted heuristic such as classic, modern, etc.
- A cognitive mode in which one thinks about the sensory, intellectual, and emotional qualities of an object, a place, or an event. In this definition, aesthetics is a way of simultaneously perceiving the world sensorially, emotionally, and intellectually, and making a map of reality based on these perceptions.

Aesthetics in this definition applies to the sensory knowledge and felt meaning that humans construct as a result of what we experience through our senses.

In both of these meanings, there are implications for important yet subtle aspects of sustainability leadership. One of these implications is that an aesthetic, in the sense of a style, does not necessarily have to be about beauty – it could be about ugliness, grotesqueness, simplicity, or functionality. For example, the aesthetic of Scientific Management is efficiency in all things – activities and operations, information, and energy use. This efficiency-based sense of style can be applied to an organization's physical surroundings such as offices, manufacturing or service areas, and the exteriors and grounds of operating facilities. The efficiency-based sense of style can also be extended to how employees dress, how they exhibit (or do not exhibit) certain mannerisms and formalities, as well as both the appearances and functionalities of the products and services produced by the company.

Another implication is that the predominant organizational aesthetic will influence how people experience the company's operations, products, and services. The more clearly expressed and defined the style of the organization is, the stronger the experience will be for stakeholders. Leaders that wish their company to be in business for an extended period pay close attention to the aesthetic principles embodied in its operations as well as its products and services. Aesthetic considerations place a special burden on leaders: the need for understanding both timeless principles and culture-bound definitions of beauty as well as how to translate these into interesting and pleasurable experiences for organizational stakeholders both inside and outside of the company.

The user experience of a product's aesthetic characteristics has been mastered by Apple in both its products and in its retail stores. The company's products are noted for their curved lines, ease of use, simplicity of function, an uncluttered window into the operating system, and pleasant tactile sensations. One of the core marketing approaches of Apple is to offer a multi-sensory experience that drives customer delight and loyalty. The product and store designs encourage users to interact with the computers while having fun and feeling good doing so, the goal being to deliver an enriching experience for all customers.

A third implication is that a leadership aesthetic is developed over time through exposure to and immersion in specific sets of social surroundings. Leaders, as do all people, can change their aesthetic criteria over their lifespans as their social surroundings change. These criteria come from their families, communities, peer groups, and society at large, and form what can be called an aesthetic sensibility. From the perspective of the Thousand Year Model, leaders learn about aesthetic criteria from immersion in their communities, as well as learning from positive relationships with stakeholders. Leaders ensure that the development of aesthetic criteria remains synchronized with larger social realities through these two mechanisms.

From a sustainability viewpoint, it is important to note that an organizational style or sensibility is an essential aspect of its organizational identity. This identity is expressed in the branding of products and services, the actions and appearances of managers, the roles and functions of employees, and the organizational communications with stakeholders. Similar to the synchronization of aesthetic criteria, identity synchronization creates social legitimacy and ensures the company a place in society as a respectable and desirable business citizen.

From both aesthetic criteria and identity integration we can understand that the aesthetic aspect of sustainability leadership must necessarily involve the management of meaning through the manipulation of forms, symbols, and stories, which are predicated on the development of both leader and follower aesthetic perspectives. Since people generate meaning through their sensory perceptions, it is a primary job of leaders in a sustainable company is to encourage their followers to develop their own aesthetic awareness by supporting their personal development. In this way, leaders help followers attune themselves to the primary organizational culture and style. Since employees want to be a part of organizations that appeal to them on aesthetic dimensions, leaders must first define and actively create their own aesthetic sensibility, make sure that their sense of style is reflected in the organization, and then attract employees who resonate with this particular style. Apple again comes to mind, as the company selects people for its retail outlets who have a strong desire for excellent customer service, a passion for the company's products and services, and now with the release of the Apple watch, a strong sense of fashion and style.

A developed sense of aesthetic awareness is also important for followers because it provides them with the capability of interpreting the messages crafted by the leader. Without such a capability, the subtleties and implications of the leader's messages will not be fully comprehended (at the least), or quite possibly entirely misunderstood. These messages are especially important when it comes to issues of facility, product, and service design. Without an aesthetic awareness, employees will exhibit a kind of tone deafness when it comes to the design processes of the organization and how the results of these processes are affecting both their own and their customers' lives.

The goal here is to create an informed experiential knowing in each organizational member.

Another reason for developing the aesthetic discernment skills of followers is that these individuals will be more aware of their surroundings and the events transpiring within these surroundings. Followers will see, hear, and sense more and will engage with situations often before problems exist. They will gain a higher tolerance for ambiguity and tend to question assumptions being made in decisions and prior to executing tasks. Such questioning is a mark of reflective intelligence, which greatly benefits any organization by providing feedback on decisions and actions, enhanced consideration of alternatives, and a buffer to prevent unacceptable consequences. In terms of innovation and improvement, individuals with a highly developed aesthetic sensibility tend to be more curious with a high desire to formulate hypotheses about ambiguous situations, which can form the basis for effective actions.

An example of a company based on the high level of aesthetic awareness of its employees is the Zildjian Cymbal Company. The company has been in existence for almost 400 years. Indeed, for Zildjian the level of employee aesthetic awareness is a core competitive advantage that has been passed down through generations of owners and craftsmen. The cymbals are made from alloys of copper, tin, and traces of silver and even platinum that are mixed together to create a unique sound and a beautiful visual appearance. The specific methods of mixing the metals and finishing for sound quality are closely held secrets first discovered by the company founder Avedis Zildjian in 1623, and passed down through successive generations of managers and craftsmen. The result, however, is that Zildjian cymbals are renowned throughout the world as the best available.

Employees involved in manufacturing are trained in the proprietary mixing and finishing processes and thus gain the skills necessary to create the clear and brilliant sound of these musical instruments. The aesthetic is both visual and sound-based, and is the basis of the manufacturing process that creates the sound, weight, and visual qualities of each instrument. Some of the employees have been with the company for more than fifty years and have developed a keen sense of the aesthetic necessary to distinguish Zildjian cymbals as a unique musical product. The company remains committed to integrating its aesthetic as the core of its quality management system, and to continuing to produce world class musical instruments.

Regardless of the level of aesthetic development of followers, the leader's efforts will define the aesthetic dimensions of working life presented to employees and other stakeholders. The organizational architecture – its structure, working environments, myths and stories, and visual images – all affect the emotions and thoughts of followers to a degree commensurate with the level of the follower's aesthetic sensibility development.

The design and development of an organizational architecture is the sole purview of leaders, who in effect define the nature of the society in which employees will live while laboring for the company. It is the particular ordering of these elements that gives any company its unique character, and for a sustainable company, these elements will be arranged in a manner designed to encourage awareness of interconnection with the world as well as feelings of positive connection to the organization based on experienced meaningfulness. Ultimately, satisfaction with work life is tied into whether or not employees sense that they are producing something that resonates with their personal aesthetic sense and to some degree is a thing of beauty. An example is the lobby of the Zildjian Company with its historic drum sets from famous musicians like the Beatles along with stories of the company's history. Employees pass through this area and are reminded daily of the prevailing company aesthetic as well as the historic, social, and artistic significance of their work.

From a customer viewpoint, aesthetic leadership is absolutely essential for the economic success of any company. Aesthetic considerations for products and services are part of every customer experience. Whether absorbed subconsciously or developed as part of a structured learning process, all people have a set of aesthetic criteria with which they express themselves, and which act as filters for their sensory perceptions of the world. All customers, regardless of their level of aesthetic sensibility development, perceive products and services sensorially, emotionally, and intellectually. Since it is a truism that people are attracted to and desire to possess what is beautiful, when an individual interprets an object or an experience as beautiful they will seek to possess it, safeguard its vitality, and preserve it from degradation. Thus, products and services that reflect a socially-defined aesthetic of beauty will be highly sought after by customers.

Jonathan Ive, Apple's leader of industrial design and human interface, has developed a world renowned aesthetic for the company's computers and phones. His aesthetic has tapped into people's need for a simpler way to live in the face of the growing complexity of modern life. Apple customers are willing to stand in line, camp out overnight, and even travel thousands of miles to purchase the company's products. Ive leads a team of industrial designers who create the "emotionally warm modernism" of the company's products, and describes his aesthetic as follows:

Simplicity is not the absence of clutter, that's a consequence of simplicity. Simplicity is somehow essentially describing the purpose and place of an object and product. The absence of clutter is just a clutter-free product. That's not simple.

Two important operational considerations for organizational leaders are the alignment of the company culture with the culture of the society in which the company operates, and the creation and communication of symbols, stories, and myths that reinforce the company culture. Leaders following the Thousand Year Model will act on ever deepening stakeholder relationships to develop a sense of the core beliefs and values on which society operates, and on which the company culture should be based. Taking care to reflect deeply, leaders in a sustainable company will develop a keen sense of how to balance what matters in society with the set of universal human needs addressed by company operations. When what matters to society is translated into symbols, stories, and myths, the result is a unique expression of a company style based on a specific time, place, and technology.

In terms of stakeholder linkages, sustainable companies pay close attention to the aesthetic criteria present in the environment. Elements such as contrast, economy of features, integration of form and function, balance, harmony, and interdependence all arise from close observations of the natural world and its multitudinous non-human life forms. Leaders will strive to build a culture that appeals to and promotes the positive emotional connections to the natural world that most people possess, and that emphasizes an interconnectedness of life approach to organizational style, structure, and operations. Finally, leaders will strive to emphasize the importance and power of individual responsibility in protecting the natural resources upon which the company depends for its existence.

There are three levels of aesthetic practice for leaders. In the first level, the expression of style is through simply decoration or adornment of objects, facilities, and behaviors. The underlying style is perhaps not clear or is different from the embellishments being made. An example might be when people place Christmas decorations on their houses during the annual holidays.

At the second level, leaders go beyond mere decoration and strive to create the setting in which followers can enter into a unified experience of a whole. Discrete elements of a facility, product or service, or behavior are put together in a way that signifies a distinct style. Efforts here are in the realms of department store window displays, hotel lobbies, clothing designs, and the emerging field of virtual reality. The goal is to structure mutually reinforcing sensory inputs in all modalities that create a unique and pleasing experience while stimulating imagination.

Finally, at the third level, leaders move beyond decoration and experience into transcendence. In this area, leaders seek to create the beautiful within an experience of wonder, reverence, awe, and delight. Leaders operating at this level of aesthetic awareness will create artifacts or experiences that seem to freeze a moment in time, taking followers out of the here and now in recognition of timeless universals. Some examples might be a masterpiece painting by Picasso, the great cathedrals of Europe, immersion in one of the theme parks at Disney, or an insightful lecture delivered by a skilled orator.

Within each of these levels is an increasingly powerful leadership presence that is based on the awareness of the need to model desired behaviors. In a sustainability context, this need translates into recognition of sustainability leadership as a performing art, the goal of which is to promote a common understanding among followers of the ideas, values, and style of the organization. Leaders in a sustainable company are meaning makers, and see themselves as actors in a play whose plot is the ongoing thriving of the company throughout changing times.

Aesthetics at Keiunkan

One of the first things one notices when entering the Keiunkan lobby is the sense of refined grace that pervades the entire facility. From the second one walks up to the door and is greeted by the personal hostess, there is an overwhelming sense of restrained elegance. The primary aesthetic is simplicity based on the forms of nature. The grains of wood and stone, the lines of the building, and the clothing of the hostess all suggest the harmony of nature and culture, a balance of the rigid formality of human architecture and the asymmetry and wildness of the natural world.

Figure 8. Integration with the natural environment

The overall impression is that Keiunkan is the result of co-creation between man and nature. The building and its rooms and soaking areas, the employees, and the food all reflect smooth and graceful beauty. The restorative waters have been integrated into all aspects of the onsen seamlessly. As one enters into Keiunkan, one is conscious that the place offers life support enclosed by a sense of style and beauty.

The essence of Keiunkan is an environment that is stress-free, a haven from the frenzied activity of the city. There is a general sense of quiet and calm, an absence of loud noises, and extensive views of the river valley and its trees and rocks. Each guest has access to nature, in both the individual soaking tub in their room as well as the community soaking areas. Keiunkan offers the promise of restoration and revitalization – a renewal of personal perspective and energy. Such environments have been shown in many studies around the world to restore one's sense of themselves and their lives, and ground one in the flow of the natural world. Keiunkan is no exception, and people have been coming here for over a thousand years in recognition of the power of the place.

One senses immediately upon entering one's room that there has been very deliberate attention paid to the guest experience in all of its aspects. Outside the room is a menu written by hand and signed by the chef and the hotel manager, detailing the events of the stay and the meals to be taken. While the atmosphere is subtle and the amenities unobtrusive, every attention is paid to those elements that support the health and enjoyment of the guests. Nowhere is this attention to detail more obvious than with the food served.

The meals show a union between beauty and functionality, and are a joy to eat. Each dish has its own unique flavors and composition and is served on a small plate that complements its size and color. The food consists of items grown or caught locally. Moreover, the food changes as the seasons change, and the menu is dedicated to achieving harmony among the food, the tableware, the season, and the inn. The culinary approach amplifies simple and basic food by putting an emphasis on elegant presentation. The idea is to make a very little food go a long way by arranging sight, smell, taste, and touch so each aspect complements and amplifies the others.

Finally, the aesthetic of the inn is attenuated by the countenance and bearing of the staff. Quietly professional, the staff models an honoring of the tradition of the inn while providing extraordinary service for the present. In every gesture, the pride of serving guests as part of an honored tradition that dates back centuries is obvious. Each employee models correct manners and etiquette, and exhibits a dignity in the form and deportment of their bodies. The overall form is modesty, gentleness, kindness, and honesty with a smile.

CHAPTER 4

Managing a Thousand Year Company

From a day-to-day perspective, it is the leader's job to help managers take the long view and maintain an understanding of how sustainability adds value to the company's customers, suppliers, and other stakeholders. Leadership comes first – without strong leadership, managers can be tempted to take shortcuts which may yield a short-term boost in performance but undermine the long-term viability of the company. Leaders serve as the proxy for feedback loops on the long-term performance of the company. They align the elements of the organization so that over time the organizational efforts are balanced and focused on achieving the company purpose. Without strong leadership, sustainability management simply does not make any sense.

In this chapter, we review the management processes that are necessary to build an organization that thrives over time. Keep in mind that managers must pay attention to how they are implementing these processes and assess their success in each area of the business. Planning, budgeting, developing structures, staffing these structures, and monitoring the results are all necessary in each area of endeavor.

In the Thousand Year Model, the management of a business is defined according to six distinct areas of emphasis. Each area represents an integrative process, and the model discounts traditional groups such as Marketing, Accounting, and Operations in lieu of functions that support the long-term success of the company directly. The presupposition is that it is more important to directly manage and support what an organization does to be successful over time, rather than develop silos of activity that require extensive coordination and tend to run to their own agendas.

Although the Thousand Year Model contains six distinct management elements, in reality these elements are interlinked strongly through leadership. While each element indicates an area of a company to which attention should be paid by managers, no element exists entirely in isolation from others, and changes in one element inexorably affect other elements. For example, learning about a new scientific advance from a conference (Integration) might result in more focused technology development and refinement of an existing core technology (Learning). At the same time, the amount of resources invested in the development would be constrained by the financial position of the company (Control), as well as the new technology's effects on customer value (Integrity) and a need for new training (Mastery). These interrelationships become more visible in the following explanations of each management element.

Focus on Customers: The Process of Integrity

One of the most important factors for the success of any business is how customers experience a company's products and services. As part of normal use, the customer experience determines whether or not customers will make one or two repeat purchases, become loyal over an extended period of time, or move beyond loyalty to become in effect ambassadors or evangelists for the company, touting its products and services to their friends, families, and communities. In today's business environment, especially with the onset of online shopping, the customer experience is becoming an important if not primary factor in gaining a competitive advantage.

Stepping back and taking a wider view, it becomes clear that an excellent customer experience is obtained as an output of the process of integrity. This integrity process consists of four linked activities:

1. The identification of the human needs that the business addresses
2. The explication of those needs and a set of core values in a documented credo
3. The development and reinforcement of a brand that reflects the core values
4. The realization of the brand value as part of the customer experience

These elements and an overall view of integrity are shown graphically in Figure 9, below.

Once the leadership defines the purpose of the company, managers can establish the linkage to human needs. In fact, all valid organizational purposes are based on the fulfillment of one or more human needs. As can be seen in Figure 9, once the company purpose and human need fulfillment are defined, human need satisfaction can coalesce into a customer experience. However, in order for this coalescence to take place, managers must link the company purpose to specific human needs the company addresses in both a credo and a brand, and use this brand to define the characteristics of all customer interactions with the company's products and services. The process of integrity converts abstract values into both customer perceptions and concrete experience.

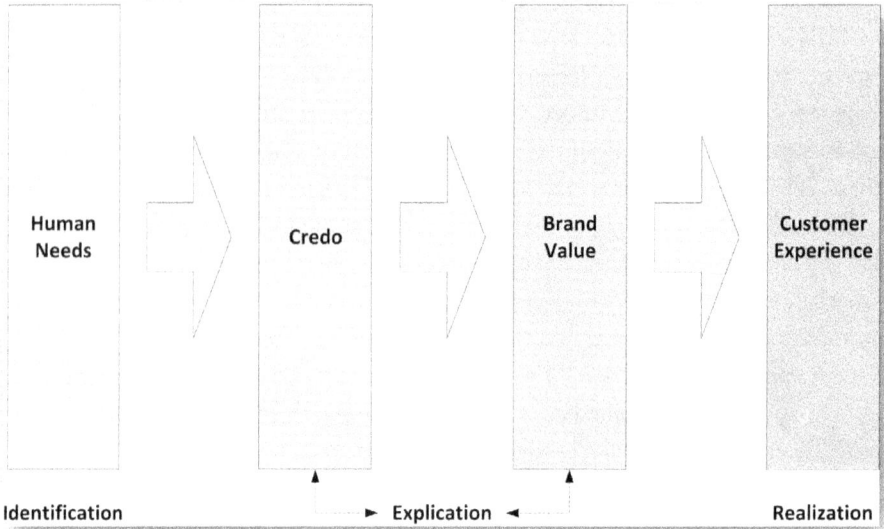

| Human Needs | | Credo | | Brand Value | | Customer Experience |

Figure 9. Integrity overview

Regardless of what purpose drives a sustainable company, all purposes are linked to the fulfillment of one or more human needs, and sometimes fulfill several simultaneously. From the inception of the company, a critical concern of both leaders and managers is that their products and services must be perceived by customers as valuable. Such perceptions are reinforced when customers can clearly understand why a company was formed, and how a company's products and services will help them to solve their problems and meet their needs.

The linkages between purpose and human needs is a bedrock for the company – the fulfilled needs support what business the company is in and its reason for existing. We can better understand human needs by considering a taxonomy of human needs that was introduced by the Chilean economist Manfred Max-Neef in his book *Human Scale Development*, and which is presented in Table 6.

Need	Satisfiers
Subsistence	Physical and mental health, supported by food, shelter, and work
Protection	Care, adaptability, safety, savings, social security, and equilibrium supported by health systems, social security, family, cooperation, living space, and gainful employment
Affection	Self-esteem, respect, tolerance, generosity, and passion supported by friendships, family, partnerships, and relationships with the natural world

Understanding	Critical conscience, curiosity, discipline, and rationality supported by literature, teachers, and schools
Participation	Adaptability, receptiveness, solidarity, dedication, and involvement supported by rights, responsibilities, duties, and privileges
Idleness	Curiosity, sense of humor, and tranquility supported by games, spectacles, clubs, parties, and peace of mind
Creation	Passion, imagination, inventiveness, and curiosity supported by abilities, skills, and meaningful work
Identity	Sense of belongingness, differentiation, self-esteem, self-image, status, and assertiveness supported by symbols, language, religion, reference groups, values, and norms
Freedom	Autonomy, self-determination, open-mindedness, rebelliousness, and tolerance supported by equal rights and responsibilities

Table 6. Typology of Human Needs

Source: Adapted from Max-Neef, M. A. (1991). *Human Scale Development* (pp. 32-33). New York: The Apex Press

The usefulness of this taxonomy for building a sustainable company is threefold. First, this set of human needs is universal and has appeared consistently across time, space, and different countries. However, the ways in which human needs are satisfied has differed according to the different cultures and different technological ages in which an organization exists. A given human need was met very differently in the feudal societies of the past than it is today. Each successive culture determines the specific technology, structures, institutions, and systems through which a universal set of human needs is met. As Sheldon Kopp, the psychotherapist and author, said, "The answers keep changing. The questions remain the same."

Second, this taxonomy is non-hierarchical and non-exclusive. This means that one, two, or several human needs can be met simultaneously through one type of action or process. An entrepreneur interested in starting a sustainable business can select specific needs to be met based on their observations of what needs are not being met currently in the markets and in society generally. Also, managers wishing to make their business more sustainable can assess their linkages to this set of human needs.

Finally, this taxonomy offers a clear basis on which a company can build a credo. The purpose underlying a company's existence is most often reflected in a credo – a simple statement of purpose linked to one or more human needs. In essence, a credo can be viewed as a proposition that contains implicit beliefs about what need is important while defining an operating purpose for a company. A credo can act as a guide for company actions and management decisions, and can be combined with a company mission, although it does not have to be.

The first step in managing the integrity process is to define the linkage between the company purpose and human needs. There are several need-based considerations that managers should mull over. These considerations include how the proposed products and services will impact the Earth's ecosystems, how communal spaces to promote interaction and participation will be provided, and how processes, time, and facilities for innovation and creativity will be provided during regular working hours. The goal here is to make sure that the company's business model avoids products and services that provide short-term benefits but incur long-term costs that exceed those short-term benefits.

The second step in the integrity process is to include and explicate the fulfillment of human needs in a credo, which is linked closely to the company's purpose. Usually, a founder's vision and purpose will be expressed in a credo and honored over time. Sometimes a credo can be the same as a company purpose, while in other cases it can include an additional explanation. A credo does not have to be long or complex, but it does need to be capable of being internalized by employees and becoming part of the brand definition and customer experience. For example, Keiunkan's credo is a collection of sculpted images with auspicious meanings, and is shown in Figure 10. At the center of the visual credo is a happy and vitalized person, surrounded by arrows, cranes, turtles, pine trees, sake drums, and carp, which have the following meanings:

- Arrows: focus on achieving goals
- Pine: endurance, steadfastness, and positive energy in times of misfortune
- Cranes: longevity and good luck
- Carp: prosperity and success
- Turtle: long life
- Sake drums: opening to harmony and good fortune

Figure 10. Keiunkan's visual credo

Company	Credo
Apple	In everything we do, we believe in challenging the status quo. We believe in thinking differently.
Disney	We use our imagination to bring happiness to millions of children and families throughout the world.
Merck	To preserve and improve human life.
Southwest Airlines	To give the common man the freedom to fly.
Charles Schwab	We are relentless allies for the individual investor.
Pivot Leadership	By helping leaders be their best, we can create a better world.
Keiunkan Onsen	To provide a sanctuary for human revitalization.
Tellari	We are dedicated to building a better future through understanding.

Table 7. Examples of Credos

The examples of credos shown in Table 7 provide clear values that can be translated directly into a brand image. Brand alignment is one of the core competencies of sustainable companies. Many long-term companies have succeeded in building on the owner's credo, mission, or purpose statement to create a set of carefully tended values and beliefs. It is these fundamental values and beliefs that are preserved and passed down through time to all employees and managers, and that form the basis for the business brand.

According to the American Marketing Association (AMA), a brand is a "name, term, design, symbol, or any other feature that identifies one seller's good or service as distinct from those of other sellers." The AMA definition of the branding process goes further:

"A brand is a customer experience represented by a collection of images and ideas; often, it refers to a symbol such as a name, logo, slogan, and design scheme. Brand recognition and other reactions are created by the accumulation of experiences with the specific product or service, both directly relating to its use, and through the influence of advertising, design, and media commentary."

A brand can be one of the most valuable intangible assets of a company, as it can create lasting impressions in the minds of customers and other stakeholders who come into contact with the company. A brand anchors customer perceptions of value in a set of benefits that meet or exceed customer needs. At the end of the day, a brand is a set of psychological perceptions that reside in the minds of customers and other stakeholders. These perceptions inform a person about a product or company – who it is, what it does, and why customers should care. These perceptions also guide a customer to think, feel, and act in certain ways when they come into contact with the company or its products.

The assortment of brands adopted by sustainable companies is as varied as the companies themselves. The key here is understanding that sustainable companies all have one common practice around their brands: they practice brand reinforcement, which has three parts.

- *Part 1:* The company conveys the brand meaning and identity consistently to stakeholders. Every interaction with the company, no matter how seemingly small or trivial, is viewed as an opportunity to reinforce brand values and create a strong brand representation in the minds of stakeholders. This is essentially a leadership task.
- *Part 2:* The second part of brand reinforcement is based on the founder's credo and business purpose. Sustainable companies are able to articulate the purpose clearly and succinctly, and make it a priority to adhere to this purpose throughout all phases of operations. Additionally, the sustainable company focuses on its core values and makes sure these values are assimilated by every employee and reflected in every stakeholder interaction.
- *Part 3:* Strongly link the brand realization to human needs. Through formulation of a credo and forging brand distinctiveness based on the core human need being fulfilled, a brand gains its power. Employee awareness of the human need being fulfilled creates both motivation and deep sense of purpose, which serve as guideposts for decision making.

The final link in the integrity process is the customer experience of the company. Christopher Meyer and Andre Schwager, experts in the field of customer experience management, define customer experience as "the internal and subjective response customers have to any direct or indirect contact with a company." Customers of sustainable companies should experience authenticity, trust, and reliability when encountering the company and its products. The goal is for the customers to realize an embodiment of the core values as expressed in the credo and brand while gaining the personal satisfaction that their needs are being met and their problems are being solved.

The difficult part of customer experience management comes with making sense of the customer touchpoints to the company. While customer experiences with company products and services are relatively easy to define and manage, the multiple touchpoints for customers form what Alex Rawson, Ewan Duncan, and Conor Jones refer to as the *customer journey*. Customer journeys take place when new customers are brought into a company, customers make repeat purchases or upgrade services, or even depart the company.

When we view customer satisfaction as the net result of all of the customer interactions with the company, we have defined the outcome of the customer journey. Managing the customer experience requires not only identifying each touchpoint, but also linking them together so that the company provides an integrated approach to a consistent experience and consistent satisfaction levels.

The linkages required to deliver a consistent experience will involve different groups within a company, such as sales, customer service, operations, design, information technology, and even human resources. The implication of this involvement is critically important: not only must there be a defined set of customer touchpoints, but also these touchpoints need to be managed in a way that brings together each affected group around a common set of core values and a well-defined brand image.

A simple yet powerful example of a customer journey can be found in the Murakami-Ju Company in Kyoto, Japan, which has been making more than twenty varieties of pickles for the past 180 years. Murakami pickles are an example of what is known as Kyoto cuisine, and are made with fresh seasonal vegetables cured through simple methods and minimal flavorings. The proprietary manufacturing process uses hand-picked ingredients like salt, rice bran mash and vinegar that enhance the flavor, color, and texture of the locally grown vegetables, and no artificial colorings are used. The result is a delicious and unique taste that cannot be replicated by other companies.

Pickles are a core part of the Japanese diet, and Murakami pickles can be found in department and grocery stores throughout the country. Such locations are the first touchpoint for customers, and the brand identity is defined by the family crest on the packaging as well as the delicious fresh flavor of the pickles. Enclosed with the package is a small history of the company, establishing it as a keeper of Kyoto's traditional cuisine. The company tradition is as much a part of the food as the pickles themselves.

The next touch point is the company website, where the company history is presented and pickles can be ordered as gifts for delivery throughout Japan. Murakami pickles are seen as part of the country's cultural heritage, and are much prized as gifts. The third and final touchpoint is the shop where the fresh pickles are sold, and which is the front for the pickle factory in back. The outside of the shop displays both the family crest and the name of the company in a simple and distinctive style. After passing through the doorway, one enters the tasting room and sits on benches that have been worn down by thousands of visitors through the decades. The visitor is greeted by the friendly and courteous staff, and is offered a set of small cups containing the juice from the latest batches of pickles. Finally, after one has selected their purchase, the pickles are wrapped in a distinctive packaging marked with the family crest, ready to be carried to the visitor's home.

The company focuses and aligns its integrity process and customer touchpoints seamlessly. The pickles fulfill a need for garden-fresh, nutritious food. The company credo is based on upholding the tradition of Kyoto cuisine, which involves unique and creative ways to prepare delicious food. The brand value is both the wonderful flavors of the pickles as well as the historical tradition of the company. Finally, the company has managed its touchpoints such that the brand value – uniquely prepared delectable food that is part of the creative and historical Kyoto tradition – is realized throughout the customer journey.

As a management priority, the important point about integrity is that it is concerned primarily with alignment and traceability. Beginning with the defined human need and business purpose, there must be clarity in the explication of the credo and the brand. This clarity should be expressed as criteria for managing the customer touchpoints in the context of a customer journey. A lack of clarity at any of the first three stages will result in a less than optimal customer experience, as will an overly complex credo. Alignment goes hand in hand with simply stated, clearly articulated, and well-formed customer outcomes.

Extensive diversification into related and unrelated businesses is a danger to integrity. As a company grows, the natural tendency is to expand into different business lines and different markets. Sustainable companies, however, remain highly focused on a specific market niche and do not allow dilution of the core values or brand image. Managers implementing integrity define a set of clearly articulated values that meet human needs and that are reflected in the brand, the customer experiences, and in leader behaviors. Straying from these values is simply not done. Although technologies may change and markets may grow and shrink, the sustainable company will remain centered and limit their growth to a size appropriate for their needs fulfillment, credo, and brand value. Time and time again we have seen companies grow to huge sizes only to eventually collapse under the weight of administering their complex systems as well as the inability to manage different lines of business simultaneously.

A second danger is loss of the positive reputation of the company. Managers strive to keep all customer experiences as well as the net result of customer journeys positive. A positive reputation is supported by high product and service quality as well as the tradition of providing high quality

consistently over time. While this function was performed in the past by individuals concerned with public relations, today the emergence of social media has necessitated the involvement of the broader function of media relations.

We can think of integrity as a sports car, powerful and fun to drive, but prone to crashing unless the driver maintains control over all that power. The strength of the integrity process comes from two factors: alignment and focus. Sustainable companies align their customer needs, credo, brand promise, and customer experience using a clearly defined set of core values. The implicit assumption is simplicity: these core values are few in number, which enables them to be internalized by employees as well as easily experienced by customers and other stakeholders. As in the Murakami example, when the integrity element is focused and aligned, its power to guide the company is realized fully.

An important concomitant product of integrity is organizational culture. The integrity process, when executed effectively, provides the values, beliefs, and norms that form the basis of an organization's culture. However, these values, beliefs, and norms are necessary but not sufficient for creating a culture: also needed are leadership actions to develop the culture's strength within the company. The integrity process provides the content of culture, and the mastery process along with leadership power imbues the company with a strong culture that allows for process simplicity and employee empowerment.

The Principles of Integrity
1. Company leaders model core values to maintain consistency of internal and external stakeholder interactions
2. Company leaders strive to uphold a positive reputation
3. The brand has a strong appeal to a well-defined niche
4. The brand is linked directly to human needs, company identity, and customer value
5. The original brand is maintained as a source of tradition and legacy
6. A unified business identity is reflected in the company credo, brand, and customer experiences
7. The credo is documented and reflects core values clearly

Table 8. The Principles of Integrity

Integrity at Keiunkan

Keiunkan's purpose is clear: to provide a sanctuary for restoration and revitalization. This purpose is reflected by Yuji Fukazawa's frequent statements about the inn to his employees, and his use of a visual representation of the credo displayed in the lobby. Yuji is a living reminder of what the inn is all about and why it exists, and his decisions reflect a consistent perspective of both time and purpose. He is also the primary spokesperson for the inn, representing it in all interactions with local communities, media, and local governments. He holds the reputation of the inn as part of the brand message and uses the tradition of the inn as part of the value proposition for customers.

The inn's reputation has been enhanced by achieving the Guinness World Record for the oldest hotel, yet Yuji has not used this as point of pride; instead, he uses it to invoke a sense of tradition and enhance the Keiunkan brand appeal. The Keiunkan brand is linked directly to the human need for physical health. By providing a place firmly ensconced within both Japanese cultural history and the natural environment, Keiunkan is seen by customers as both a living tribute to the value of longevity and sustainability as well as actively supporting human vitality.

The continual remodeling of the inn serves to reinforce a unified business identity that is a model of the cultural traditions of Japanese lodging. In the past thirty years, more than $25 million USD has been invested in renovating the facilities to reflect both comfort and traditional styles. Artifacts of these traditions are found everywhere, from the tatami mats, to the futons for sleeping, to the meals created entirely from local foods. The managers at the inn go to great lengths to make sure that the guest experience is seamless from start to finish, and each guest is surrounded with an atmosphere of relaxation, refinement, and rest. This business identity has a strong appeal to those individuals and families that seek a unique restorative experience far away from the hectic city life, an experience that is both steeped in the traditions of centuries as well as reflective of a vibrant presence today.

Finally, the physical location of the inn is a core part of the customer experience. The inn is located in a remote village in the Minami Alps, far from the noise and distractions of crowded cities. This location promotes an atmosphere of peace and quiet, which is important for relaxation and restoration. The physical location is a highly noticeable part of the brand message, as guests can sense they are entering into a truly different time and place when they stay at the beautiful location of the inn.

Fiscal Conservatism: The Process of Control

The purpose of control in any business is to make sure that performance meets standards set by management. In most organizations, these standards are economic as well as behavioral standards for employees. In this particular area of sustainability management, we emphasize control of finances rather than control of employee behaviors, which are managed through succession planning, mastery training, skills development, and organizational learning. While some sustainable companies may choose to implement employee performance management and control systems such as segregation of duties, physical access, and limited authorization, the heart of control for sustainability remains monitoring the financial aspects of the business closely.

The key goals of financial control in a sustainable company are threefold:

1. To create the ability to fund operations during fluctuating cash flow situations including economic downturns
2. To balance operational funding with capital investments for the future
3. To identify the risks that affect present and future cash flows

A sustainability-based approach to financial control is centered on (a) identifying points in the company's operations where internal financial controls are important, (b) generating relevant financial information on a regular basis, and (c) protecting the company's financial assets. Leaders strive to be aware of the cash needs of the business by measuring financial data and taking action to make sure that a conservative financial policy is implemented throughout the company. Cost controls are implemented as necessary to maintain standards for financial activities.

An important part of the control in sustainable companies is the management of risk. Most of us are familiar with the application of actuarial tables in the calculation of insurance policy premiums. This quantitative approach to risk has been used successfully for many years and enabled numerous insurance companies to thrive. The quantitative approach, however, tends to be rather complex and calls for a specialized set of statistical analysis skills. When we look at sustainable companies, we come to realize that their approach to risk is very different and is not, for the most part, quantitatively based.

From a sustainability viewpoint, risk is best defined by the International Organization for Standardization (ISO) standard 31000. The standard defines risk as the following:

Risk is the effect of uncertainty on objectives. An effect is a deviation from the expected – positive and/or negative. Objectives can have different aspects (such as financial, health and safety, and environmental goals) and can apply at different levels (such as strategic, organization-wide, project, product and process). Risk is often characterized by reference to potential events and consequences or a combination of these, or may be expressed in terms of a combination of the consequences of an event (including changes in circumstances) and the associated likelihood of occurrence.

The degree of formalized risk management varies with the specific business; however, formal risk management in sustainable companies is always present to some degree. The two primary components of a sustainability-based approach to risk management are (a) identification and assessment of stakeholder trends and events likely to affect the company, and (b) maintenance of a conservative financial position to ensure the availability of financial resources that will enable the company to withstand any changes, seen or unforeseen, that might arise from these trends. Risk management is directly related to stakeholder integration, as it is the set of stakeholder relationships that provides necessary information about the changing world and its implications for company managers. Risk management is also integrated, as it covers financial, quality, environmental, and health and safety risks.

The financial management emphasis in a sustainable company is on cash flow. Rather than seeking growth first, managers will look to optimize cash flows from operations. Profit is important, but is not primary. Instead, profit is viewed as a lagging indicator of a well-run company. In order to maximize profit, a sustainable company will focus on operational efficiency and adopt a conservative financing position. Such a position involves (a) keeping debt levels low or nonexistent, (b) maintaining low fixed costs, (c) seeking favorable credit arrangements, and (d) offering flexible customer financing options. The emphasis on operating efficiency involves areas such as core work processes, inventory management, and distribution. Debt is approached as a necessary evil, and the best financial terms are sought for any money borrowed.

One area where fixed costs are not necessarily minimized is employee salaries. This is where we see a balance between control and employee mastery. A sustainable company will pay its employees much higher compensation than competing companies as managers strive to build and maintain core operational knowledge within the company. This building process means keeping people from leaving, and above average compensation is one method of doing that. Sustainable company managers view higher salaries as a necessary cost of doing business and retaining key employees, and establish fair remuneration policies appropriate to each person's contributions and responsibilities.

An aspect of this compensation approach is to link compensation to business cycles. This linkage means that when the company does well, all employees share in that good fortune and increasing amounts of cash are accumulated in the business. When the company encounters lean times, rather than reducing headcount, the sustainable company managers seek to maintain full employment by lowering all salaries and other fixed costs as well as engaging people in non-productive work, such as facility maintenance. This downturn approach links employees to the financial returns of the company directly, and allows employees to experience a greater sense of ownership in the company outcomes.

Profits and revenues in the sustainable company are not seen as ends in themselves, but are viewed as outcomes from substantive social, ecological, or technological accomplishments. Profit supporting survival is seen as the one of the keys to success for the long term. Managers seek a balance between profit and sustainability. To achieve this balance, cost reduction measures are implemented to the degree that they begin to impact stakeholder value, and managers seek to prevent reduction of that value. In other words, financial costs are reduced to the lowest point possible without affecting how different forms of value are generated by the company through its operations.

One of the challenges of cash flow management is reinvesting for the future. This is where the form of company ownership comes into play. Managers in the standard form of publicly-held corporations are required by law to maximize share price, and have limited options when it comes to making major investments that affect cash flow, dividend policy, or owner's equity. Other forms of ownership are more conducive to sustainability, and a company that is owned privately such as a Limited Liability Company, Professional Corporation, Benefit Corporation, or a family-owned company has much more flexibility when it comes to making major investments. A company wishing to be sustainable should adopt an ownership structure that allows for maximum flexibility for long-term investment decisions that keep cash within the company so this cash can be reinvested as necessary to build for the future.

In 2011 GlobeScan, SustainAbility and the United Nations Environment Program prepared a report based on the feedback from a survey of sustainability experts and industry managers. One of the most poignant findings from the survey was the impact of what they termed "financial short-termism." According to the survey,

An overwhelming 88 per cent of respondents cited the long-standing problem of financial short-termism as the most important barrier for developing sustainability focused business models. Resource scarcity is driving demand and pushing up prices. Some investors and businesses have sought to exploit these trends through speculation and hedging strategies designed to deliver quick returns rather than protecting the natural assets that business and society depend on.

Acceptable return on investment time frames vary by industry sector, for example from 12 months in the ICT sector to more than 30 years in the power-generation sector. These time frames often conflict with appropriate time frames for regeneration and recovery of ecosystems. Longer return on investment time frames are increasing, but this is not widespread.

Equally important as investment for the future is keeping cash in the business to support operations. This approach allows managers to build and maintain a large amount of liquid working capital to handle fluctuations in customer orders and the changes associated with general economic cycles. For example, the managers at companies such as Agilent Technologies, Intel, Acxiom Corporation and White Electronic Designs have lowered the compensation of employees and managers during downturns to achieve the goals of keeping everyone employed while remaining profitable to some degree. When the business revenues returned, the salaries went back their original levels.

These types of changes in compensation management go hand in hand with the modest lifestyles of sustainable business owners such as Yvon Chouinard of Patagonia. Many sustainable business managers are very comfortable with the level of material wealth their business provides for themselves and their employees, but they do not seek to increase their compensation incessantly. Rather, they prefer to provide a decent living for themselves and their families while keeping most of the accumulated wealth in the business, building it for the future.

The bottom line for control is that it enables the company managers to focus on investing for the future, efficient operations, and profitability rather than growth. The core financial strategy of any sustainable company eschews growth as the main emphasis. Rather, the primary strategic goals are (a) developing competencies to meet current and future challenges, (b) appropriate size based on the specific market niche being served by a specific technology, and (c) maintaining a conservative position to support firm longevity. As a consequence, a primary financial goal is not reinvesting to become larger, but reinvesting to develop: to keep up with the latest technology, become more efficient in its operations, and provide a high level of value for customers and other stakeholders. Money serves the purpose of getting better, not bigger, and profit supports survival, not growth.

The Principles of Control
1. Focus on longevity and cash flow management as core concerns
2. Adopt a conservative financial position by keeping debt levels low or nonexistent
3. Invest for competency development to become better at delivering value to stakeholders
4. Emphasize profit through efficiency, not growth
5. Achieve profit as a result of social, technological, and ecological successes
6. Implement fair and generous compensation policies linked to business cycles
7. Manage economic, quality, environmental, and health and safety risks to anticipate

Table 9. The Principles of Control

Control at Keiunkan

The managers at Keiunkan show both enormous flexibility and rigid control to balance their financial strategy. This strategy is not implemented as a stand-alone approach; rather, financial considerations are balanced with brand value, customer experience, and investments for the future. For example, a recent remodeling required several millions of dollars in investment. At the same time, to cover this investment the inn raised its prices for both food and lodging. Once the remodeling was complete, the higher quality guest experience provided more than enough customer value to justify the increased prices, and the percentage of return guests actually increased from 25% to 40%.

As with other operational concerns at Keiunkan, financial management is concerned with supporting the longevity of the company by providing exceptional value for customers. As was mentioned in an earlier chapter, when a landslide took out part of the road to the inn, managers lowered prices and provided transportation from a local town to maintain cash flow while retaining full employment. In other words, the focus of control is on maximizing cash flow as external events change, and on having enough of a cash reserve to be able to adapt to these changing events. In addition to building the capability to handle multiple forms of risks with a cash cushion, Keiunkan changes its rates seasonally to maintain cash flows, especially in the winter when many fear to make the journey up the river valley, as the road can quickly become treacherous. These strategies have been successful, and the inn maintains consistent occupancy rates between 60% and 80% year round.

Another core concern is efficiency, and the inn trains its staff to first focus on delivering a successful customer experience and then on improving the methods used to deliver that experience. Since staff is aware that their salaries are two to three times what individuals in comparable positions in other companies are paid, they take a high level of responsibility for their actions and are motivated to seek greater efficiency in methods and systems. In effect, the higher salaries promote a greater sense of both ownership and pride in the improvements being made to day-to-day activities.

Adapting to Change: The Process of Learning

The element of learning is concerned primarily with the management of technology. The core learning concerns for managers are (a) how to create and preserve a core technology and core business approach that cannot be imitated by competitors, and (b) how to update and modernize the technology and business approach to reflect the latest scientific advances. Managers seek to protect, preserve, refine, and enhance the core technology while adapting and extending it continually. An important implication of this effort is the need to identify a strategy for diversification into new technologies and new business models.

Managers concerned with learning focus on both the core and supporting technologies used to create stakeholder value. The core technology should appeal strongly to basic human needs, which are defined in Table 6. Managers must determine how they can link the core business technology to specific human needs in ways not done by other companies, all the while remaining true to the founder's credo and to the niche market to which this technology is being applied. The core question is this: what can we do (or learn to do) so that we can achieve the purpose for which this organization was created?

Technological excellence can be long-lived or it can be fleeting. Some technologies, such as food preparation, have remained virtually unchanged for centuries, while others such as cell phones and tablet computers, seem to change almost overnight. Success at technology adaptation depends on many factors, not the least of which is the inherent complexity of the technology itself combined with the will to master it.

One of the most important aspects of the capacity to endure change is the continual refinement and redevelopment of a company's core technology according to the latest scientific discoveries. Keeping the technology current while updating it based on recent scientific and technological advances requires not only a commitment to learning and continual improvement, but also a dedication to mastery similar to how a skilled craftsman approaches their craft. Moreover, not only does maintaining technological excellence support a resilience-based capacity, it also supports the renewal and restoration of a company's core resource – the technology that it uses to generate value for its customers and other stakeholders.

At its core, technological excellence is about performance – the ability to deliver value to customers based on what is learned from positive stakeholder relationships. Technological excellence requires renewing and restoring the core business technology based on input from stakeholders. This restoration and renewal means that managers must understand changing customer expectations, changing social norms, and changing technological advancements. Managers must then adapt to these changes by actively developing the business systems and processes. Both the business managers and employees must be highly skilled masters of their operations, preserving and protecting the core technology which is the basis of the business model. At the same time, these individuals must be willing to consider improvements to the core technology based on the most recent scientific developments.

One of the distinguishing characteristics of organizational learning is an unconditional commitment to quality, defined as meeting or exceeding stakeholder expectations for value. Technology alignment becomes important, as does a deep understanding of the linkages between technology outputs and stakeholders. Formal quality management systems may be used, but in many cases are not necessary; instead, simplification and process mastery may be substituted for detailed quality systems management.

The quality of every sustainable company's products and services is unquestioningly outstanding, and includes an unwavering management dedication to excellence and continual improvement. High product and service quality is the essence of the company's business identity, and is a primary characteristic of both stakeholder value and company tradition. The sustainable company manages quality without compromise – it is 100% committed to producing the highest possible quality of products and services using its core proprietary technology. The managers and employees are all oriented towards gaining a full operational understanding of this core technology, along with continual improvement in how it is deployed.

Sustainability managers continuously focus on raising performance standards and beating themselves using ideas from stakeholders. Although it seems counterintuitive, the idea of benchmarking is not really important. While best practices are considered, it is the development of the company's own unique solutions based on a specific tradition, proprietary technology, and unique employee skill set that is most important. The primary competitor is themselves. Increases in productivity and cost reductions are linked directly to higher employee compensation.

Preserving and improving core technological competency is a central part of the quest to improve how the company operates. In some cases, the core technology that the company is using has remained essentially the same over time, and in other cases the technology has been refined, updated, and streamlined to reflect the latest advances in science. Managers will seek to balance deep knowledge of the traditional technology and its associated products and services with new and emerging technologies, exploring the possibilities for enhancement. The commitment to traditional products remains unmoved, however, and a sustainable company will maintain its array of traditional products even if they are not profitable in order to retain customers and generate customer loyalty.

Although traditional products and processes are sustained and renewed, refinement of the core technology based on scientific advances is a strategic business imperative. Managers in a sustainable company will engage in ongoing process optimization, modernization, and enhancement to improve productivity and effectiveness. The goal is to balance deep knowledge of company and product traditions with new technologies and systems. Management systems such as corrective action will also undergo similar revisions, with the goal of preserving and enhancing the overall organizational effectiveness. The goal of such continual improvement is to enrich the products and services by building the capability to provide more value using the same or fewer resources.

A core strategy to improve process efficiency and effectiveness is the reduction of complexity by continual redesign. Processes and systems evolve over time towards increasing complexity and it is easy for managers to lose sight of the original process purpose. There is a balancing act that managers must perform with regards to technology. The continual advance of science means that new methods, new materials, and new information are being generated constantly. The challenge for managers is to adapt the existing core technology and supporting technologies to these recent developments without reducing the value that the business provides. The business must remain recognizable from the standpoint of distinctive products and services that build upon a tradition of quality, while at the same time improving the effectiveness with which these products and services meet human needs.

The primary source of inputs to process and product redesign is stakeholder interactions. Managers gain greater knowledge of possible improvements and innovations through an ongoing dialog with served markets, the scientific community, and other stakeholders. Memberships in community organizations, chambers of commerce, professional organizations, and other industry groups are fertile sources of ideas and trends as well as best practices. Integration with business partners as well as the local business community is also an important source of ideas for process and product development. The goal is to create an external learning community than can be used as a source of ideas for business development by soliciting suggestions and advice.

Unilever, a company that has made sustainability a core part of its operating strategy, is an example of state of the art stakeholder-based learning. The company has produced a Sustainable Living Plan for 2014 that outlines three broad goals: improving health and wellbeing, reducing environmental impact, and enhancing livelihoods. In addition to the three areas of sustainability-based activities under this plan, the company learns extensively from its industry partners, and it states that "by collaborating with partners including not-for-profit organizations, we can leverage skills, capabilities and networks that we do not have." Unilever currently focuses its learning activities on suppliers and distributors, and has established what it calls the global Program for Responsible Sourcing (AIM-PROGRESS), which is a "forum of consumer goods manufacturers and suppliers assembled to enable and promote responsible sourcing practices and sustainable production systems." This program includes the exchange of views and shared learning throughout the supply and distribution networks of the company. A key part of learning in this program is the collection, assessment, and sharing of "non-competitive information on supply chain social compliance performance."

Especially important for sustainability is the development of design feedback from ecological impact measurement and reporting. Since the ecosystems cannot speak for themselves, it is up to the managers of the sustainable company to become aware of the changes happening to ecosystems affected by the company's extraction of inputs and generation of products and waste. This type of ecological knowledge can be gained through active monitoring of the changes in the relevant functions of the ecosystems affected by the company's operations. The goals of ecological process and product redesign are to (a) design products and services to minimize resource use and waste generation, and (b) shift the negative impacts of company operations first into neutral and then into a positive zone, whereby the ecosystems affected by company operations are restored, enhanced, and improved by the business. These goals can be accomplished by designing energy efficient processes, simple yet effective management systems, waste-free production, and product take back mechanisms.

Protection of the technology as proprietary is also an important competitive factor. This protection can be achieved through employee confidentiality as well as legal protections such as patents and trademarks. The goals are to (a) maintain a core technology that cannot be imitated easily by competitors, (b) control all facets of that technology so it provides desired outputs, and (c) link the technology outputs with as many human needs as possible. The linkages with human needs provide a solid bulwark against competitors: the stronger and more numerous the linkages to human needs, the less likely it is that competitors will be able to copy the unique value proposition offered by the company's products and services. A unique proprietary technology linked to multiple human needs is a combination that is hard to beat and even more difficult to imitate.

Alongside protection of the core business technology comes a commitment to ongoing experimentation with new technologies and systems. This experimentation reflects the desire of managers to fulfill human needs in innovative ways while generating greater amounts of economic, ecological, and social value. Sustainability managers establish a culture and structure for their companies that encourages creative experimentation. Employees are encouraged to "give it a try," provided with the freedom to act, and supported in learning from their mistakes. Managers accept that mistakes will be made and encourage employees to take a kaizen-based approach, whereby small incremental steps on a continuing, even daily, basis are best.

"Bet the company" innovating is simply not done, as the risks are unacceptable: the company must sustain operations as a condition of survival. Instead, many sustainable companies undertake joint research and development projects with suppliers and partners. Major changes and innovations are reserved for the time of leadership succession, which is most often a generational change as well. Innovation most often centers on products and services adjacent to those already being provided to the niche market that the company serves.

However, it is also important to understand that some of the greatest successes of sustainable companies have come from experimentation, trials and errors, opportunism, and accidents. While the results are not always predictable, a culture of innovation supports these types of events. Managers keep a keen eye on these efforts and apply the results of successful experiments to modernize methods and systems and to adapt products for current use. This is where investments in new machines, systems, and processes happen, setting the stage for future success.

In addition to process and product experimentation, managers in a sustainable company continually search for new suppliers and customers. The sustainable company will seek to maintain a balance of repeat and new customers. This balance is also reflective of the higher costs to develop new customers versus the lower costs of keeping existing customers. This balance is where the importance of traditional products in maintaining customer loyalty comes in to play. The case is the same for new suppliers: existing suppliers are cheaper to maintain than to develop new suppliers, and managers seek to maintain a balance between existing and new suppliers. The important point to remember is that development of new suppliers and customers is a positive aspect of risk management, as these new entities lower the operational risks of the company.

The Principles of Learning
1. Employees exhibit an uncompromising dedication to product and service quality
2. Managers balance deep knowledge of traditional technology with emerging technologies
3. Stakeholder relationships are sources of innovation and learning
4. There is active ongoing experimentation with and development of new technologies, products, services, and products
5. Managers preserve, protect, and enhance the core business technology
6. The core business technology is linked to the credo, human needs, and brand proposition
7. The product and service offerings are: • original • cutting edge • offer superior value • support a positive reputation • are renewed on a regular basis

Table 10. The Principles of Learning

Learning at Keiunkan

The quality of the service at Keiunkan is simply excellent in all of its aspects, and is reinforced by immaculately maintained physical facilities, the power of the natural environment, and the restorative characteristics of the naturally flowing spring waters. In addition to the owner's position, many of the jobs at the inn such as operations manager are passed down through the generations so that the honor and respect given to each individual who holds that position is amplified. This honor and respect motivates an uncompromising dedication to service – upholding the tradition of the inn by providing the best possible experience for customers.

Part of the inn's learning process is achieved by assigning a hostess to every guest. It is the job of the hostess to make the guests feel comfortable, to serve the meals, to prepare the rooms for sleeping and to look after the needs of the guest. The hostess is engaged in a constant learning activity with each guest, seeking to understand their needs and making sure these needs are met. The hostess also makes sure that each guest feels welcomed and relaxed, just as if they were in their own home. The goal is to create a deeply personal connection with every guest and use these connections to expand the network of customers within the local region.

Overall, the technologies used at the inn are relatively simple and are all oriented towards the creation of a restorative and relaxing environment. These include housekeeping, maintaining the tubs, keeping the hot water pure and flowing at an adequate volume to meet all of the guests' needs, and kitchen operations. The management of these technologies can be accomplished by providing extensive on-the-job training and mentoring. However, the managers and employees must have a base set of business skills in order to obtain a job at the inn. This base set of skills is necessary so that employees can take an integrative approach to problem solving. Everyone is trained to understand how their job affects the provision of a relaxing environment and the serenity of the natural hot springs within the context of the entire organization's operations.

Yuji Fukazawa maintains close contact with the local communities, and has done so for several decades as he built close relationships with local stakeholders. He also is dedicated to learning about the latest hotel and restaurant technologies through conference attendance and professional societies, and carries this knowledge back to his employees. Part of his dedication to continual improvement was realized in 2005 when he managed an excavation that increased the water flow 25% to 2030 liters per minute.

Perhaps the greatest advantage of Keiunkan is that it is original and unique. There are no substitutes for its services – there can be only one oldest hotel in the world serving traditional Japanese cuisine made entirely from fresh local ingredients. The inn's location deep in the mountains, its protection of the purity of the water, and the excellence of the service staff all support superior value that cannot be replicated. Guests are treated with respect and caring, thus supporting the spread of the inn's positive reputation. Through the dedication of employees to continual improvement of all processes, the inn keeps its competitive edge, and a recent renovation of the facilities has created a clear connection to both the inn's cultural traditions and a pleasant and restorative guest experience.

Building Relationships and Connection: The Process of Integration

The integration element is concerned with stakeholders, those parties that have that have a stake, or some form of interest, concern, or involvement, with the company's success or failure. Managing this element is centered on two primary concerns: how a company situates itself among its array of stakeholders, and how it builds and maintains relationships with those stakeholders. The goals of managing relationships and connection are to:

1. Identify stakeholder interests and impacts
2. Implement strategies to meet those interests and create positive impacts
3. Create a positive company reputation and social license to operate
4. Develop trust by keeping promises
5. Maintain proactive learning systems based on stakeholder relationships
6. Cultivate and strengthen long-term relationships based on shared value
7. Continually increase stakeholder value

One of the most important shifts in strategic thinking that sustainable company managers make is to visualize their company as a node in a stakeholder network rather than as a stand-alone entity. This network perspective is distinctly different from an industry-centric perspective, as it allows for alignment of multiple groups with different interests and activities affected by the company operations. Rather than interactions governed solely by direct company operations or customer concerns, the sustainable company identifies relevant multiple stakeholders and actively manages the value exchange process with each stakeholder.

According to Freeman, Harrison, and Wicks in their 2007 book *Managing for Stakeholders*, stakeholder relationships are essential for organizational survival, positive reputation, and continued success. Adopting a stakeholder perspective redefines a business as "a set of relationships among the groups that have a stake in the activities that make up the business." Managing these relationships requires that an organization adopt a more widely based view of business operations that includes both active consideration and continual improvement of its relationships with its network of external stakeholders. Managers extend the traditional value chain to include multiple parties, which are selected based on the assumptions made about how these parties are impacted by company operations. Stakeholder management offers an approach for implementing social responsibility, ethical management, and ecological effectiveness, all of which lower operating risk and build trustworthiness into both short-term and long-term business operations.

The stakeholder map shown in Figure 13 illustrates the two basic categories of stakeholders for any company. The inner circle represents those likely to be affected by a company's operations in a direct manner with short feedback loops that provide information quickly. The outer circle represents those stakeholders with a less direct involvement with the company's operations and longer feedback loops. Managers in a sustainable company constantly evolve and revise operating strategies to match changes in stakeholder concerns and actions.

Implicit in this map is the element of time. While the stakeholder map is focused on the current state, it also includes (a) the future generations of people in all categories as well as (b) the past generations of people in all categories. Especially important are the founders of a company who would be considered past employees. Thus, consideration of any stakeholder's interests would take into account past, present, and future impacts on company operations.

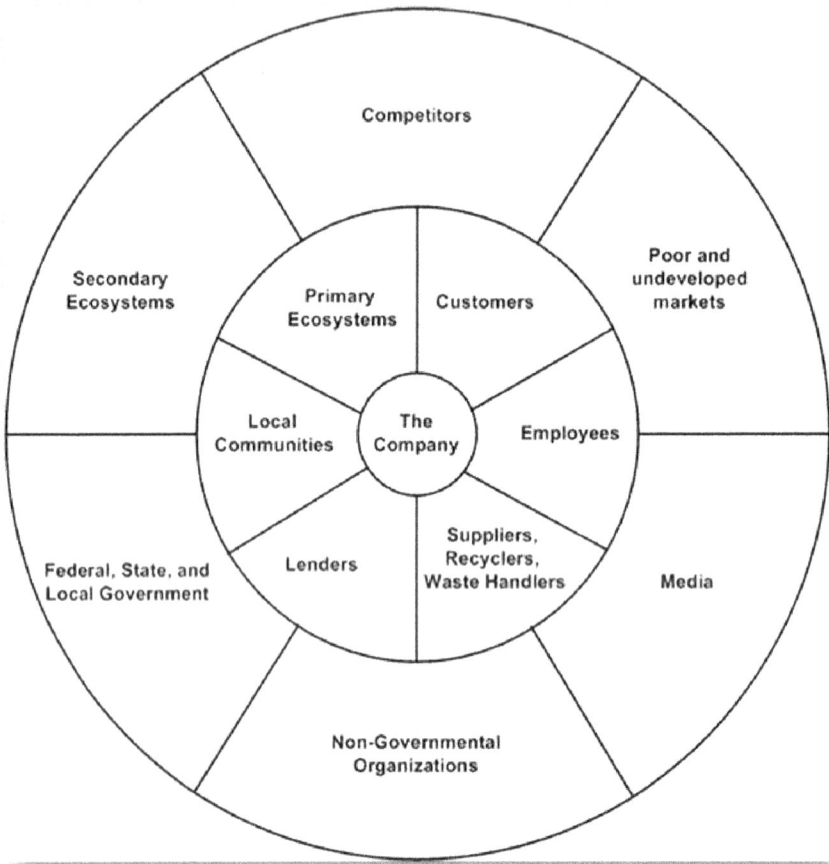

Figure 11. Stakeholder map

Source: Camarota, A.G. (2011). Exploring the elements of sustainability management in the solar photovoltaic industry. Ann Arbor, MI: Proquest LLC.

Placing an organization at the center of its stakeholders is a strategic perspective that acknowledges the network model, which establishes links to both human organizations as well as the Earth's ecosystems. It is the properties of this network model that drive sustained organizational excellence. Networks function according to interdependent change, continuous communication, and decentralized power. The important point to remember about networks is that they are essentially democratic – participation by all nodes, or elements, of a network is required in order for the network to function effectively. This is why sustainable organizations respect and defer to stakeholder interests – this respect and deference simply keep the network up and running.

Participation of stakeholders can be accomplished by a strategy that Michael Porter and Mark Kramer define as "shared value." When a company creates economic value and increases its competitiveness in ways that also advance the economic and social conditions in the communities in which it operates, it is creating shared value. A shared value strategy recognizes that costs previously seen as externalities are also internalities, imposing significant costs for the company.

An example of shared value might be a lack of effective education programs in a local community's schools, which leads to underskilled employees that require extensive training to become productive. A company located in this community has no choice but to bear the cost of this training and internalize the social cost of a poor educational system unless it contributes to its betterment. By providing cash donations, used computer equipment, meaningful employment, and encouraging employees to become mentors and tutors for the school, the company can help the school system to raise the effectiveness of its education programs. By performing these actions over time, in the long run, community goodwill will be increased, and the company's direct training costs will be decreased.

There are several important implications of this shared value perspective. These implications include the quality of the relationships formed, the ways in which value is created and exchanged, and the methods through which a company builds an infrastructure that supports stakeholder interests. Managers adopting a stakeholder strategy must consider each of these in turn, as these implications can be mutually reinforcing when managed properly.

When a company decides to set itself in its network of stakeholders and create shared value as a core operating strategy, the result is a strengthening of the stakeholder relationships. These relationships, in a sustainable company, emphasize positive emotions as well as tolerance of diverse views. Managers work to create feelings of trust, satisfaction, and wellbeing throughout their stakeholder network, and they begin this work by gaining a deep understanding of stakeholder interests and treating each one with respect. The goal of relationship management is to provide a positive and mutually beneficial set of interactions that help each party to meet their needs.

A deep understanding of stakeholder needs is particularly important in the case of customers. Managers must not base their decisions solely on their assumptions about customers, but actually learn from them, taking prompt action on complaints and concerns, treating customers fairly, and using the information gained to improve company operations. The information gained from a deep customer knowledge then becomes the basis for differentiation. Such a deep understanding cannot be obtained through mere focus groups or surveys: it must be obtained through personal relationships, in-depth conversations, and observations of behaviors taking place over an extended period of time.

In a sustainable company, managers will implement customer service programs that provide the latest product information with the intent of building close customer relationships and increasing loyalty. The goal of these programs is for the customers to become a type of partner in the business, and encourage customers to provide feedback that helps the company to find new ways of meeting their needs. This open communication and active solicitation of feedback help the company to gain both credibility and trust in the eyes of customers.

There are two goals for customer communications. The first goal is to learn from an ongoing dialog how to create shared value for customers. This means listening closely to customers and in addition to developing personal relationships use various forms of communication media. The second goal is to communicate the company story so that the brand value becomes ever more firmly ensconced in customer's minds. As the dialog continues, the company establishes itself with a clear image and identity and reinforces trust by engaging in respectful learning about customer needs and desires.

This learning approach is not limited to customers, but also includes suppliers. The sustainable company will seek to create embedded long-term ties with suppliers. Suppliers in many cases are perceived as even more important partners in the business than are the customers: they can be the source of new ideas, product innovations, and technological improvements. The sustainable company shares information with suppliers and engages in an ongoing dialog about operational needs, forming a tight integration and a form of partnership based on collaboration. The supplier network is based on the company's extensive knowledge of its products and services, which managers use to drive improvements through the supplier while collaborating to obtain the best technology and gain significant improvements.

Although existing suppliers are important, managers will seek constantly to broaden their horizons. At the same time they are working to deepen existing supplier relationships, managers will also seek new suppliers as sources of fresh ideas and new technologies. They will engage in the process of continual adaptation of the supplier network to the changing operating needs of the company. The goals are to ensure an ongoing capacity of the supply of products and services needed to maintain company operations, and to lower the risk of interrupting operations.

Along with optimizing supplier networks, sustainable company managers seek to optimize distribution networks for their products and services. According to Porter and Kramer, in many cases this optimization consists of building clusters of "firms, related businesses, suppliers, service providers, and logistics infrastructures" to facilitate the exchange of the company's products and services. An important aspect of this effort is the strengthening of the local communities in which the company operates. The concurrent optimization of customer and supplier relationships in addition to distribution networks also fosters a life-cycle perspective for managing products and services.

The local communities in which a sustainable company operates are seen not only as a source of employees, but also values and norms by which the company should operate. The company can support these communities by providing tax revenues, employment and meaningful work, involvement in local community building activities, and extensive sponsorship of local charities. The goals are not only to generate shared value, but also to create and maintain a social license to operate. Maintaining close contact with community leaders and their organizations can be facilitated through promoting employee involvement in community service programs as well as direct financial support for those programs.

The previous example of Unilever's Program for Responsible Sourcing (AIM-PROGRESS) shows how the company is dedicated to developing existing supplier relationships and optimizing distribution networks. Based on what the company terms "a virtuous circle of growth," Unilever seeks to increase operating efficiencies, eliminate waste throughout the supply chain, and use the network of suppliers and distributors as a source of innovative ideas for developing the company's products and services. The company also engages extensively with suppliers to promote greenhouse gas emission reduction strategies. In addition, suppliers are encouraged to gain an increased awareness of their social responsibilities such as the empowerment of women and human rights in the workplace. At the center of the AIM-PROGRESS program is the foundation of an ever-deepening set of stakeholder relationships.

Walden University is an excellent example of community involvement. The school has implemented a program called Global Days of Service, which consists of a volunteer force of 9000 employees that work on community service projects throughout the world several times each year. According to the company, in 2014 volunteers engaged in more than 100 projects such as collecting food, diapers, clothes, and shoes for children in Mexico; walking to increase awareness and raise funds to send underprivileged children to school in Uganda; and providing dental care for young orphans in Costa Rica.

The school takes these community service activities very seriously. Walden has made community service a core component of its mission to create positive social change throughout the world. According to Walden's published mission,

> Walden University defines *positive social change* as a deliberate process of creating and applying ideas, strategies, and actions to promote the worth, dignity, and development of individuals, communities, organizations, institutions, cultures, and societies. Positive social change results in the improvement of human and social conditions.

Walden's commitment to community involvement is an example of how to integrate community-based stakeholder relationships into the core of an organization.

Community involvement also includes government involvement, which is important for the sustainable company. Managers engage actively with federal, state, and local governments to promote the company interests as well as lobby for favorable legislation. Regulatory compliance is managed at an executive level to emphasize the important of the government relationships. The goal is to establish a stable position for the company within its applicable regulatory scheme while being an advocate for industry interests. Such advocacy can include involvement with professional societies and trade groups as well as government lobbying.

There are several important challenges associated with managing stakeholder relationships and connection. The first challenge is setting material flow and operating boundaries between the company and its stakeholders: where does the company end and the stakeholder begin? This type of boundary is especially important when managers consider the natural environment, or the ecosystem services on which the company depends for its survival. The definition of environmental impacts can be a difficult task, yet it is absolutely necessary if the company is to define the natural resources it uses and the waste products it generates. Assessing and managing this flow is crucial to establishing the company's position within a biocentric perspective. At the same time, the ecosystem services used by the company can necessitate certain elements of relevant ecosystems be included as partners of the company. This inclusion in turn requires some form of ecological restoration as a core company process for renewing essential resources.

In order to establish a rational basis for decisions about the company activities and its resource use, managers must establish the company's operating boundaries. When extensive and embedded partnerships with suppliers and customer are created, the company boundaries can become blurred. It is up to the managers to form a cohesive organization that can clearly identify who are its members and who are not, and protect its proprietary technologies. While decisions are made with both suppliers and customers as key concerns, ultimately the interests of the company and its survival must take first place.

The second challenge for integration is to develop learning-based relationships with all human stakeholders, including customers. This development means approaching stakeholders with humility and respect, and understanding clearly how the company's products and services are designed to meet human needs. The goals of learning-based relationships are to create engaged communication with customers and suppliers, and address the concerns and needs of other stakeholders. Integration requires the active involvement of managers in order to learn from stakeholders what their interests are, how the current products and services offered by the company meet their needs, and what more can be done to meet or exceed their expectations. Integration breaks down into four processes:

- Identifying important stakeholders
- Engaging with these stakeholders to determine how they are impacted by company operations
- Developing strategies that ensure these impacts are positive
- Maintaining learning-based relationships to co-create solutions based on changing interests and conditions

The quality of relationships is an especially important strategic choice. Once the managers in a sustainable company have identified the set of relevant stakeholders for their business, they need to define the level of interactivity and power allocated to each stakeholder. The range of relationships is from powerful – where the stakeholder is a partner in the company – to merely passive, where the company engages in one-way communication about company events. The managers of a sustainable company should determine where the relationship with each stakeholder should fit in the typology shown in Figure 14 based on the objectives of involvement. Not all stakeholders require a high level of involvement, and managers must be careful to surface and challenge their assumptions about what level of involvement is appropriate. The important point here is that managers in a sustainable company must select a stakeholder strategy based on how the maximum level of shared value can be obtained for each stakeholder.

Stakeholder Control	**Stakeholder Power**
Partnership	Approaches: • Proactive interactions • Multi-way dialog
Delegated Power	Tools: • Community projects • Board representation • Joint ventures • Strategic alliances
Involvement	**Stakeholder Tokenism**
Negotiation	Approaches: • Responsiveness • Constructive dialog • Reactive bargaining
Consultation	
Explaining	Tools: • Questionnaires • Focus Groups • Task forces • Advisory groups • Workshops
Placation	
Informing	**Stakeholder Non-Participation**
Therapy	Approaches: • One way dialog • Public relations
Manipulation	Tools: • CSR reports • Briefing sessions • Leaflets, Pamphlets • Magazines, Newsletters • Other publications

Company

Stakeholders

Relative Power,
Degree of Involvement

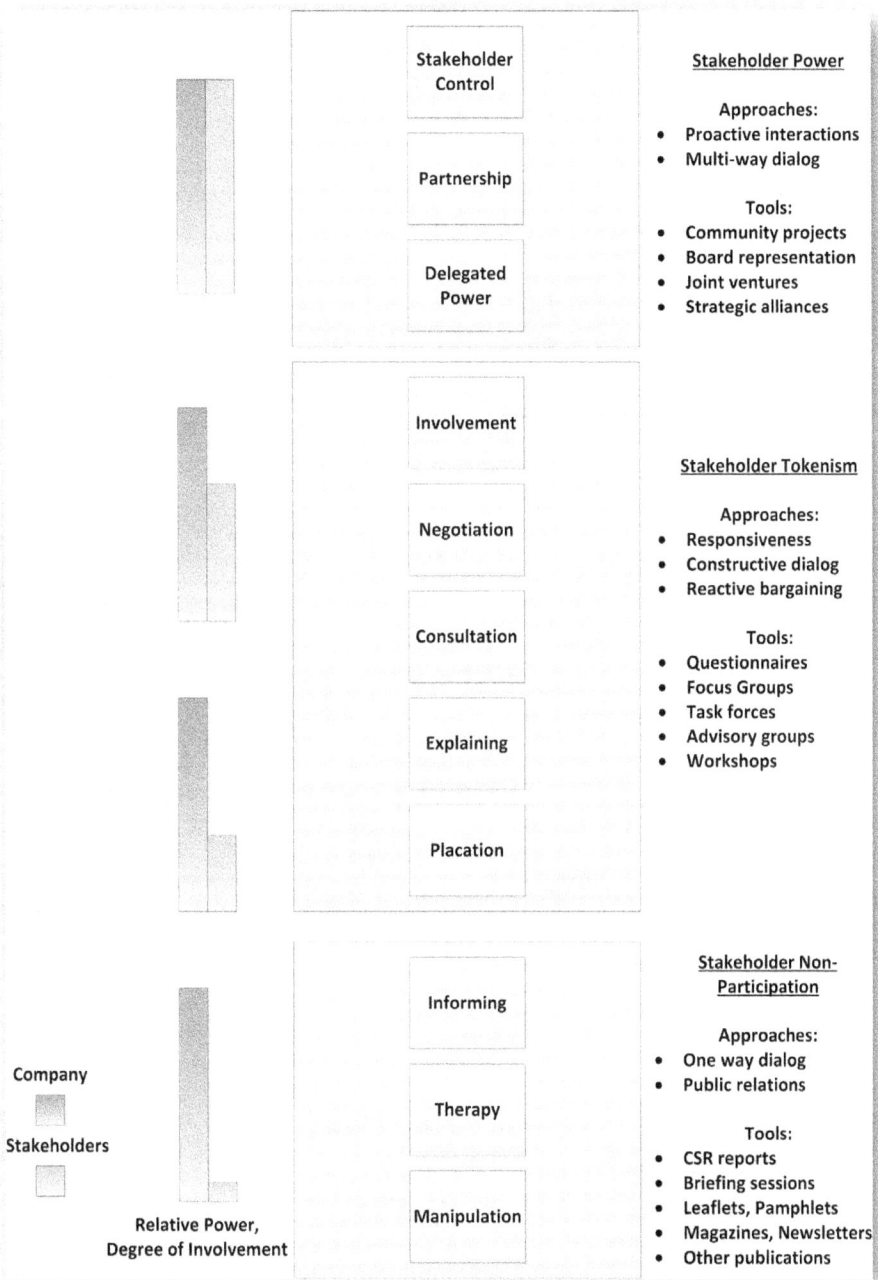

Figure 12. Stakeholder management typology

99

Adapted from "Stakeholders: Theory and Practice" by A. Friedman and S. Miles, 2006, Oxford University Press, and "A Ladder of Citizen Participation" By S. Arnstein, 1969, American Institute of Planners Journal, 35, p.217.

In order to assess its positioning among its stakeholder networks, the sustainable company has some form of measurement for determining its social legitimacy as well as the value being added to all stakeholders. This form of measurement can be formal or informal, quantitative or qualitative, extensive or limited. The important points are that (a) the company's ecological, social, economic, and technological performance is known, and (b) shared value generated as a result of stakeholder relationships is identified as used as part of continual strategy development.

The Principles of Integration
1. Extensive local community involvement and support
2. Identification and management of ecological impacts
3. Identification of stakeholders and their relevant interests in company operations
4. Development of shared value strategies for each stakeholder
5. Cultivation of trust-based long-term stakeholder relationships
6. Active government involvement through compliance and lobbying
7. Development and maintenance of a positive company reputation
8. Creation of close embedded ties to suppliers and customers
9. Development of customer and supplier loyalty
10. Managers and stakeholders are aware of what the company is doing operationally as well as for its stakeholders

Table 11. The Principles of Integration

Relationships and Integration at Keiunkan

Yuji Fukazawa has extensive personal ties to the local community that he has developed during his many years living there. He actively recruits and selects employees from the people living nearby, including their friends, families, and visitors. The relationships with employees are marked by respect, higher than normal wages, and an employment situation that includes living quarters and meals as well as a salary and benefits. The managers aim to instill a sense of pride in each employee that stems from contributing to an honored tradition as well as delivering outstanding service in a restorative environment. Employee welfare comes first, and is the basis of everything that happens at the inn. Yuji realizes that the way in which customers are treated is a direct reflection of how employees are treated, and that building a culture of service excellence starts with treating employees well.

One of the most visible aspects of the connection to the local community is the food served to guests at the inn. The food is selected by a highly experienced and trained chef, and is drawn exclusively from local farms. This means that the managers must maintain close and long-standing ties with local farmers and other food suppliers. The local food is an important part of the brand appeal and is featured widely in brand messages. Guests know that they will be fully immersed in a restorative and relaxing environment and that the water and meals they consume will be both aesthetically pleasing and healthful. The local food also adds a visceral element to the experience, as guests can physically consume both the spring water and the local foodstuffs, literally eating the environment.

The menu and the tradition of the inn are used as the content of messages to all stakeholders, and along with the commitment to service excellence form the basis for a positive reputation. Yuji has created a tightly focused message based on cultural tradition, and spreads this message with the intent of making the inn a symbol for the entire region. The message has resulted in a positive reputation throughout Japan, and is the basis for extraordinary customer loyalty – more than 40% of the guests are repeat customers.

Special attention is paid to the natural environment, as the waters are the essence of the restorative experience. The managers have built the facility so that there is a constant and adequate flow of water to all rooms. The water is used for everything without being treated – drinking, bathing, showering, and toilets – because it is so pure. Yuji interacts regularly with all stakeholders involved with maintaining the pure water supply, including local governments, contractors, employees, and the local ecosystems, which he supports by planting trees and restoring the mountain soils. The goal of the inn's relationship with the natural world is to renew and restore the ecosystems in which the inn is situation and on which the inn depends for its livelihood.

Yuji is also involved extensively with local governments and construction firms. As part of this interaction, he is concerned with and has promoted the construction of a tunnel and a new road to the inn. Not only do this tunnel and road make it easier for guests to travel to the inn, it eases the transportation burden for the local communities as well – the very definition of shared value.

Commitment
& Change

Control

Integrity

Leadership

Integration

Learning

Mastery

Honoring the Past and the Future: The Process of Commitment and Change

The primary theme of commitment and change is moderation. Through moderated change, the managers in the sustainable company make sure that the organization develops and maintains the capacity to endure changes in its operating environment. Here we see the balancing of two seemingly opposed needs: the ability to change rapidly in response to significant external events, and the ability to maintain the integrity of the core business model. Too much change and the company risks losing focus and diluting its value-add proposition; too little change and the company risks stagnation and obsolescence. The goal is tempered change, change driven by relentless experimentation and learning and restrained by formal governance and career progression structures.

Governance

This element is strongly linked to the other elements, yet contains a few distinct practices not found elsewhere, such as having a defined strong governance structure that ensures continuity of business processes and keeping a business within the family. Such a governance structure would utilize an oversight board similar to a board of directors, consultants, and advisors. In a family-owned business, this would include non-family members to increase the objectivity of the governance process. An effective oversight board could be as simple as one or more mentors, or it could be more formalized as in a corporation. The goal is the same: obtain steady guidance from a set of experienced business managers, and apply their wisdom to day-to-day operations. Such a governance approach is crucial to the long-term success of any sustainable business.

Career Path

In addition to a governance structure, stability and modulated change are provided through a defined career path within the company. Every employee and manager knows how they will progress in terms of responsibilities, compensation, and authority. The formation of such a career progression structure ensures that the core business operations will remain functioning at an optimal state. In addition, a structured career path helps a company to attract and retain talented individuals because these people know how they can advance their accountabilities and compensation within the company. In addition, a structured path makes it easier for managers to define succession planning in all phases of the business. Perhaps most importantly, the structured career path can serve as a communication tool to help everyone in the company understand how they are contributing to the overall success of the business.

A structured career path is can also be a tool to develop competent leadership within the company. Effective leaders need to have a broad understanding of company operations as well as a deep understanding of the business model and credo. Such a dual understanding can be achieved by moving leaders through a series of positions that allow them to run many of the company operations, and gain an understanding of the problems involved in daily activities.

Innovation

The active side of change is also important. This side is characterized by strong commitments to experimentation, to learning about the latest scientific advances, and to advancing the core business technology to keep current with the latest developments. Management must understand and control the core technology using the best tools and materials available as well as adopting any relevant methods and process used in other organizations. Sustainable managers will commit to learning about potential new methods for achieving the same or better results, and then incorporating these methods as a part of an overall innovation strategy. Experimentation means that managers allocate resources for research and development, and assign the process of innovation an important place on the executive agenda.

A prerequisite for innovation is the establishment of a learning culture within the organization, which is directly related to a sensitivity to the stakeholders and the external operating environment. Such a culture is based on information sharing, operational transparency, and good communication. Managers can promote such a culture by establishing a positive, cooperative, and safe working environment for their employees. Commonly experienced learning activities in such an environment would include active recognition of internal and external problems, solicitation of ideas for improvement, and exploration of possible solutions for problems posed by stakeholders. However, from an adaptation management perspective, the aim here is to not merely communicate openly, but to identify both potential and actual drivers of change for the company. Such drivers could include social trends, emerging Internet memes, natural or man-made disasters, changing competitor stances, and globalization. Management seeks to learn about drivers of change, assess the impacts of the change on the organization, and then take actions to increase positive impacts and decrease negative impacts.

Change-Based Culture

There is another aspect of moderation that is critical for a company's survival: embedding the processes of change and risk management into the organization. This means that, regardless of how a sustainable company has gained a competitive advantage, it always practices change management and risk management to some degree. Change and risk management act as centrifugal governors, regulating the resource flows and business activities so the company does not grow too large or too fast, and is capable of withstanding significant fluctuations in the economy. Companies that lack such governance mechanisms invariably come apart or cease to exist. Change in this context supports the fundamental objective of survival.

Survival is also the core value underlying the orientation of the company managers towards achieving an appropriate size. Rather than a primary commitment to unrestrained growth, the core company commitments are to reach an appropriate size, fulfill the development potential of the organization and all of its individual members, and have everyone be as good as they can be at living the credo and fulfilling the company mission. Managers seek to fit the optimum pace of growth to the relevant industry sector changes and to the development of necessary management competencies. In other words, the managers seek to maintain a size of the company for which their competencies are adequate, that enables their customers to be provided with consistently high quality products and services, and that supports the brand value by introducing the element of scarcity.

Technology Adaptation

A sustainable company achieves moderation in the realm of change by balancing tradition and emerging social values. These emerging values become apparent through the cultivation of learning-based stakeholder relationships, which can also serve as a means to spot and capture sales opportunities. There is another aspect of moderation here: managers seek to change gradually in order to maintain the integrity of the existing stakeholder relationships. The goals are to remain focused on the business on which the company's reputation rests and be true to the company credo while innovating based on emerging values.

From an operational continuity standpoint, managers will seek to continue to serve a niche market based on the core technology, credo, brand, and employee skills. In response to scientific developments, the specific methods and tools used to serve the identified niche markets will change over time. In other words, managers seek to enhance the brand value obtained from traditional business practices while changing operations to survive the technological and social shifts in the societies in which the company operates. In practice, this means that managers take an aggressive stance towards technological change, encouraging experimentation and requiring a kaizen approach to continual improvement. Such technological changes are monitored to make sure that the core company values are protected and preserved as any new technologies are adopted.

An excellent example of maintaining the balance of a core technology while adapting it to modern scientific developments is the brewing industry. Some of the oldest companies in the world, such as Weltenburger Kloster and Weihenstephan, have been brewing beer according to their secret recipes for a thousand years and more. Over the centuries, these companies have maintained their quality by faithfully implementing brewing techniques and recipes passed down through the generations.

The advent of the Scientific Revolution of the early 18th century changed the industry. The invention of the steam engine and its concomitant machinery led to what is known today as automated process control, whereby machines perform the stirring, mixing, filtering, and pouring operations instead of monks laboring by hand over huge vats. These machines gave more precise control over the brewing process, enabling greater quantities to be made while holding fast to each specific recipe. For hundreds of years, most brewing, especially in Europe, was done at warm temperatures. In 1871, the invention of machine-based refrigeration enabled brewing operations to go on all year. Refrigeration machines also enhanced the control over the fermenting process by maintaining an optimum temperature for the yeast and avoiding the heat extremes that gave beer unpleasant flavors. Finally, the discovery of micro-organisms by Louis Pasteur enabled brewers to gain precise knowledge about their manufacturing processes. Brewers could now create pure yeast cultures developed for specific fermentation characteristics such as time, flavor, and efficiency. At the core of every modern brewery today is a microbiology laboratory.

The inventions of the Scientific Revolution have enabled the rise of large breweries that distribute millions of gallons throughout the world as well as the 3,400 microbreweries operating in the US today. While technology has refined the methods of beer production and distribution, these methods, along with the recipes used to create the beers, although better understood, have not changed in some cases for centuries. Brewers have learned to integrate modern process and biological technologies into their operations, which has given them more precise control. These modern technologies have also enabled a profusion of beer flavors and types in the microbreweries, unleashing the creativity of the brewmasters.

Yet all these disruptive changes have not altered the basic makeup of the product: beers today are for the most part delicious beverages with pleasantly intoxicating effects that lubricate a variety of social settings. Very old breweries have maintained their historical traditions, including specific beer recipes, as core elements of their brands and product experiences. The quality and distribution of beer have improved, yet the flavors and types of modern beers have in many cases remained unchanged for hundreds of years.

Succession and Change

A strategy for managing long-term change is associated with leadership succession. In most sustainable companies, leaders have a long-term tenure and basically are appointed for extended periods, such as fifteen to twenty-five years. Such extended terms encourage leaders to become stewards of the company and adopt a long-term perspective. However, leadership succession is always defined. Major leadership changes are deferred to a generational change, the retirement of the older leaders, and the installation of the next generation of leaders.

This strategy of generational leadership change is essential for the success of any sustainable company. Each successive generation of humans is programmed with a new set of values distinctively different in certain ways from the preceding generation. This programming takes place as a result of imprinting, modeling, and socialization and is essentially complete by age twenty or thereabouts. Thus, within a sustainable company, significant change is always generational change, and is associated with the onboarding of a new generation of company leadership that may possess a new set of values and attitudes.

Minor changes, including improvements made as a result of the kaizen process, are accomplished on an ongoing basis. These minor changes are accomplished rapidly, and are known as "first order" changes because they do not require a change in management's core values, beliefs, and worldview. Major changes, also known as "second order" changes, occur much more slowly and are associated with generational changes in leadership. These second order changes can involve a change in management's core values, beliefs, and worldview. However, even with second order changes, managers in the sustainable company will hew to the founder's vision and credo, and will explore ways in which the company can realize that credo and vision in their world.

There are two methods of change present in the sustainable company: continual small changes to adapt to shifts in the operating environment and to optimize processes and systems, and long-term major shifts in company focus and technologies that center on new ways to provide value to stakeholders with new systems and processes. These methods are shown in Figure 17. The company learns and adapts through quick, small everyday changes, and flourishes by realigning itself through slow long-term changes. These two methods of change ensure stability and moderation, and eschew "bet the company" changes and excessive risk taking.

At the core of commitment and change is a belief that the managers and owners are stewards of a treasure, a treasure that supports the survival of the company and all of its stakeholders. The owners and managers are there for the long haul and are committed to the continuing existence of the company. The managers have a long-term results orientation, and are driven by the company credo, mission, and values. They cherish the business, invest in it for long-term viability, and manage it for the long run.

The Principles of Commitment and Change
1. A formal governance structure is defined and implemented
2. An appropriate size is maintained
3. Managers create a culture that honors company traditions and learning about current best business practices
4. Managers balance short-term and long-term changes
5. Career and leadership successions are defined
6. Tradition and core values are balanced with innovation and experimentation

Table 12. The Principles of Commitment and Change

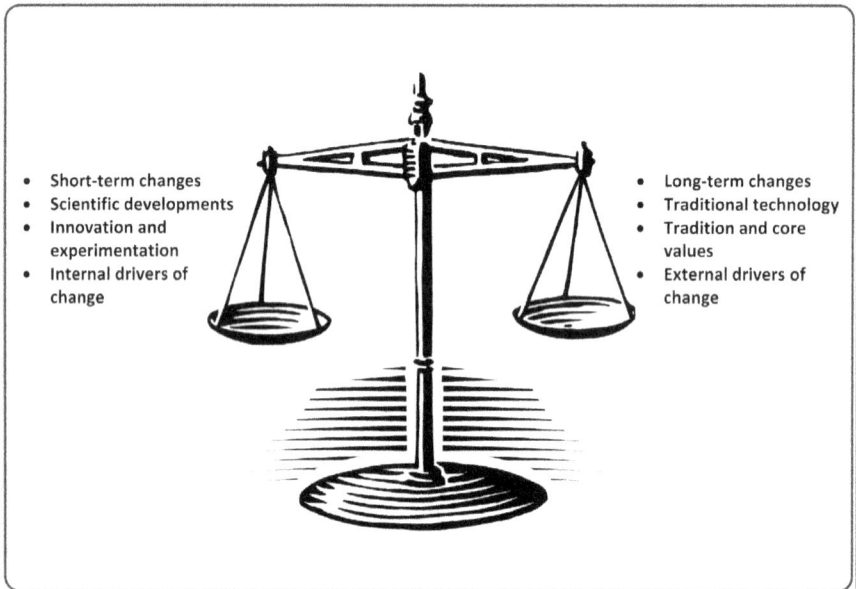

Figure 13. The balancing aspects of short-term and long-term changes

Commitment and Change at Keiunkan

As was discussed previously, Keiunkan has invested heavily in the past thirty years to renovate the facilities to gain increased guest comfort and a clearer reflection of Japanese cultural traditions. An interesting aspect of this renovation is counter-intuitive, however. Rather than increase the number of rooms available for guests, the number of rooms has actually decreased while the number of annual guests has gone down slightly. To compensate, Yuji has raised the room and meal rates accordingly. These actions are a demonstration of a commitment to honor and enhance the restorative atmosphere of the inn by creating an old-style traditional Japanese interior supported by aesthetically pleasing meals prepared from fresh local food. At the same time, Yuji has eschewed growth, and instead has kept revenues the same or slightly increased them through increased prices. By exhibiting a strong commitment to the tradition of the longest lived business in the world, the inn becomes a scarce resource with high value and thus supports the higher prices. At the same time, the renovations demonstrate an unwavering commitment to continually improving the guest experience.

Two primary goals of the inn are to meet the survival needs of the owners and staff, and to serve a defined customer niche with a high quality experience. Remaining at an appropriate size requires that the inn deliver high value for the guests, which is accomplished by a highly motivated and trained staff. The positions at the inn are well-defined, and some positions have been passed down through successive generations of the same family. Employees filling those positions are thus imbued with a sense of honor and respect for the tradition of the inn as an integral part of the job. Such honor and respect also means very high levels of employee engagement – employees are not merely pleased to perform their jobs, but consider it an honor to serve the higher purpose of upholding the tradition of the inn.

A core part of every job, however, is a commitment to continually improving the processes at the inn by eliminating waste and using fewer resources – becoming more efficient. Such improvements require that employees experiment with new methods. The inn has established a close relationship among the employees and supports their efforts to always be better. While most of these improvements are operational improvements in efficiency, Yuji and his executive staff are responsible for strategic changes such as major renovations, pricing, and facility design.

Being All We Can Be: The Process of Mastery

Mastery, according to the Merriam-Webster Dictionary, means "possession or display of great skill or technique." In a sustainable company, mastery consists of the sum total of the explicit and tacit knowledge, skills, and abilities of employees. Mastery involves both protection of the company's core technology from imitation or appropriation as well as skill development. From a management viewpoint, employee knowledge, skills, and abilities are a core component of both the social and technological capital of the sustainable company, and must be preserved and protected in order to survive over the longer term. The management approach is to develop employees to the level whereby they can do something that cannot be imitated by others.

Employees of a sustainable company, rather than being viewed as a cost, are seen by managers as the core of competitive capability. Managers understand that the overall emotional energy and motivation of employees determines to a large degree the company's continuing success, and employees are considered a fundamental asset. Again, we see that the element of mastery has two parts: the simultaneous realization of individual achievements and the advancement of organizational accomplishments. The implication of managing these two parts is that a sustainable company is best served by having its employees align their personal values with the values of the company.

Employee engagement driven by meaning and values is a non-trivial issue. A recent Gallup poll found that 70% of US employees are disengaged at their jobs as a result of a lack of shared values, costing companies $550 billion in lost productivity. Sustainable companies recognize that establishing a set of shared values as a core component of the hiring process. A state-of-the-art hiring process based on shared values is practiced by Johnson & Johnson, which was incorporated in the State of New Jersey in 1887.

Johnson & Johnson treats potential employees according to the values in its credo, which boil down to these core values:

- Committed to caring
- Responsible to our communities
- Ready to apply our knowledge and know-how
- Unique in our background and experiences
- The drivers of our own success
- Passionate about doing what's right

Everyone that Johnson and Johnson interviews is treated with respect because that projects the core value of caring. According to the Director of Recruiting, respect includes open sharing of a candidate's chances – and forms a longer relationship. The company keeps candidates informed of their status throughout the interview process, which includes a series of competency-based questions intended to elicit core values.

The interview process is structured to determine that the potential employee has both the skills to do the job based on their education, training, and experience as well as the motivation to perform based on shared values. Recruiters take the time to develop a personal relationship with the high-potential candidates, and decide if they want to be an advocate for each candidate. Advocacy is the basis for further interviews: only when the recruiter has decided that there is a shared values match does the candidate continue in the hiring process.

When employee value alignment is managed proactively through an extensive hiring process and furthered by extensive socialization, then what is important for each employee can become the same as what is important for the organization as a whole. This alignment also means that traditional forms of control are not necessary, as everyone is trusted to act in the best interests of both themselves and the company. Such alignment does not merely happen by itself – it is the result of an extensive socialization process that begins even before an employee is hired.

As we noted in a previous section of this book, sustainable companies are driven by their credo: the core purpose is everything. The business works to fulfill the credo while remaining a profitable and economically viable enterprise. This purpose becomes part of the hiring process and one of the criteria for choosing employees. Managers in a sustainable company seek to hire the best in terms of attitude, education, and business experience, and looks for individuals who have a sincere passion for making a substantive contribution to stakeholder welfare.

In addition, managers search for individuals based on the degree to which they share their core values with the company's core values. The higher the value alignment and the stronger the match, the more desirable the employee. The selection process should also exploit a potential employee's personal motivation to create something beautiful, good, and constructive. Finally, the hiring manager must make sure that there will be a good match between the opportunities available in the company and each individual's knowledge, skills, and abilities.

During the employee selection process, relevant industry-specific external experience is a crucial factor. Some long-lived companies have a policy that any leadership candidate must have a minimum of ten years of outside experience before being employed with the company. It is this outside experience that can serve as a basis for continually improving the skills and ideas used to govern the company, a method of remaining current with its management practices and technologies, and a technique for refreshing the skill base of key employees and managers. As such, a diversity of experience and gender equality is sought to create "better memories of the future" that will enable the company to expand its range of choices in its decision making processes.

Another important criterion for selection is employee education. Individuals with more formal education are sought not for the specific knowledge that they have gained through their classes, but because successful completion of their degree programs indicates that they have the ability to learn. This ability to learn is one of the core competitive advantages of a sustainable company. Given the high levels of stakeholder interaction required to gain new ideas and spot trends that may impact the company, the ability to learn is a necessity.

Once desirable employees are identified and brought into the company, managers begin an extensive socialization process. This process is based on the company purpose, and is aimed at indoctrinating employees with the company core values and credo. Managers engage in powerful socialization processes to make sure everyone internalizes the core values, and to inculcate a sense of unity and togetherness.

An important part of this socialization process is to foster dedication and commitment to continuing the company legacy. The success of this process is determined by the degree to which employees become champions and advocates for its traditions. Being a company champion means that these individuals need to feel that they are fulfilling customer and other stakeholder needs by upholding the traditions of the company. In addition, champions must experience a sense of personal achievement from living their values as a part of their work. Each champion and advocate must be absolutely clear on why they are working at the company, how working there helps them become more of who they are, and how working there helps their customers to lead better lives.

One of the most important supports for champions is the organizational culture. Sustainable companies all share a few highly reinforced values, which include the following:

- Trust
- Unity
- Fairness
- Involvement
- Commitment
- Engagement
- Enthusiasm
- Community
- Harmony
- Collaboration
- Cooperation

Effective sustainability management requires that the employees not merely know the company mission, but internalize it and become the company mission in all that they do. Employees should also trust one another as a result of forming extensive social bonds. As a part of culture building, managers can encourage loyalty, personal initiative, and cooperation to achieve the credo and the strategic goals. Bureaucratic rules, complex processes, and financial incentives are secondary in importance and are even detrimental in the longer term. The managers should strive towards unity and harmony based on respect and personal freedom, and emphasize building constructive relationships based on open communication.

Financial incentives, while secondary, are still important. In a sustainable company, employees will receive above average compensation, and make two to three times as much as individuals in comparable positions in other companies. Supporting this above average compensation is the practice of retaining employees even during economic downturns – employee retention is a central goal of managers. Having retention as a goal acknowledges the importance of preserving both explicit and implicit knowledge critical for the success of the company.

Employees are not viewed as a variable cost to be adjusted as necessary. During periods of lowered economic activity, managers will keep employees on the payroll and have them execute a variety of non-productive tasks, including facility maintenance, process redesign, or strategy development. However, alongside this retention practice is the practice of shared pain, which most often involves reduction of everyone's compensation so the company can survive financially when cash flows are reduced. Once cash flows are restored, compensation is returned to previous or even higher levels. These actions let employees know that managers believe that everyone is in this together, and foster a sense of camaraderie and solidarity because all employees are sharing equally in the both the company's success as well as its misfortunes.

Culture and financial incentives are self-reinforcing mechanisms. Managers trust that, having socialized their employees into what is important and having aligned the reward systems to reinforce those items, the employees will use their creativity, initiative, and problem solving skills to act in the best interests of the company. The success of such an approach is measured by (a) high retention levels, (b) transparent, constant two-way communication, (c) open data flows, and (d) fact-based decision making. Managers say to employees in effect that we want you here as part of our company, we are going to give you the information and tools you need, and we trust you to make the choices that are the best for everyone involved.

In addition, culture and process simplicity are also self-reinforcing mechanisms. When a strong company culture has been established, employees do not need extensive and detailed process instructions that tell them how to do their jobs. The cultural values, beliefs, and behavioral norms guide all important decisions instead. Without a strong culture, process complexity tends to increase and becomes a substitute for knowing how to make choices that reflect the best interests of the company. It is impossible to foresee all of the decisions that have to be made by all employees, and thus a detailed set of process instructions becomes a self-defeating mechanism in the longer term and becomes unable to adapt to the changes required for effective management. A strong culture allows for the maximum empowerment and employee discretion based on trust, and enables processes to remain as simple as possible.

Here is the mastery bottom line: sustainable companies view employees as human beings with physiological, emotional, intellectual, psychological, and spiritual needs. Rather than exploiting people in the short run to lower costs and drive profits, sustainable companies invest in their employee knowledge, skills, and abilities to retain them over the long term. In the sustainable company, people are viewed not merely as tools that are used to achieve profits, but as human beings that form a living community with a strong culture that reflects positive values. The company expects employees to stay with the company and make meaningful contributions over the span of their careers. Rather than simply a place to work, managers and employees take their jobs personally and feel a sense of ownership in the results of their efforts. The managers and employees also embrace mutual responsibility for outcomes: managers trust that employees will do their best for the company, and employees trust that managers will look after them and help everyone live well together.

Extensive development and training to build skills for the future is another essential element of mastery for both employees and managers, and is the basis for an orderly, rule-based, and structured career progression. The commitment to continual improvement appears again as a part of this progression, as does the commitment to grow managers from within the company. The objectives are (a) to refine and improve the set of employee knowledge, skills, and abilities that will enable the company to adapt to external changes, and (b) to manage for possible futures by investing in everyone's skills. Imbuing all employees with good basic business knowledge is a must. All employees of a sustainable company know the basics of how the different elements of a business should function, and how these elements actually function in their current company.

Not all training and development in the sustainable company is formal. The managers extend opportunities for socialization to foster informality, a sense of community, and to build strong social bonds. Rather than being seen as slacking, employee time spent building relationships is seen as essential for the company's success. Such informal socialization can take place either within the confines of the workplace or at offsite events. Through the closeness of these bonds, managers seek to reinforce a sense of elitism, of belonging to something special that is unique in the world.

A part of the training and development effort is the establishment of a clearly defined set of roles and responsibilities that are understood by everyone. This establishment does not necessarily imply a structured hierarchy with detailed job descriptions, but simply requires a well formed set of responsibilities for decision making. The purpose is to make known to everyone how they can advance in the company in terms of gaining greater skills, more accountability, and better compensation. Clearly defined exit routes are also important, as these routes enable employees to change career paths without undue hardship should they find themselves no longer served by being a member of the organization, or should they find themselves not on board with the values of the company. These exit routes empower employees to make a conscious choice to remain with the company and support its efforts, or to leave and pursue other opportunities.

Individuals chosen as executive leadership successors are given special consideration, as they are important for the long-term success of the company. These individuals receive extra in-depth socialization in the company credo, values, and mission, as they will serve as a model of these items for all other employees. The experience requirement for these individuals is even higher than for regular employees, as their knowledge of management methods will someday be critical for the company's success. However, such future leaders are required to "start at the bottom" and work their way through the entire spectrum of jobs before assuming an executive leadership position. Working through the company in this manner enables leaders to balance the process view and the goal view of their company.

The core mastery strategy for any sustainable company is to obtain employee loyalty. The first support for this strategy is creating a meritocracy rather than a bureaucracy. The second support is making strong development and learning processes available to employees so they can move through the company while enhancing their skills and knowledge. Finally, having the executive leaders be responsible for helping employees to discover the meaningfulness of their jobs is critical, as it sets the tone for mutual commitment to the company's key goals. This responsibility has a very important implication: employees are the first priority in all decisions. In short, managers of a sustainable company pay their employees more than other companies, give them better benefits, train them intensively, think of them first, and consequently retain them longer. These managers understand that how they treat their employees is how their employees are going to treat their customers and other stakeholders.

The overall goal of managing mastery is for the company to obtain a stable group of motivated, enthusiastic, committed, loyal employees who act in the best interests of the company. This group understands at a deep level that pursuit of the company mission has intrinsic value. Each employee will feel that they are privileged to be a part of a company that is making an important difference in their lives as well as in the lives of its stakeholders. Such employees do not need to be micromanaged but can be trusted to make the right choices when confronted with difficult decisions.

We know that mastery has been implemented successfully when positive psychological states have been achieved. These states allow employees to realize their potential through their work as well as be aware of their contributions are meaningful in the context of the overall company's success. The following are a set of measurement criteria that can be used to determine successful mastery implementation:

- Employees have the self-confidence to take on and expend the effort necessary to succeed at challenging tasks
- Employees are optimistic about succeeding now and in the future
- Employees persevere towards goals and redirect their actions as necessary to achieve those goals
- Employees overcome problems by sustaining their efforts and bouncing back from adversity

When mastery is achieved through a company, a flat, non-hierarchical structure best suited for adaptation and learning can be adopted. Such a structure can be kept simple and any type of bureaucracy can be avoided. Such a simple, non-bureaucratic structure supports people taking initiative when decisions need to be made and actions need to be taken, as there is no complex set of approvals that must be obtained. Employees are free to follow the values and a few simple rules in order to fulfill the purpose and mission of the company, and managers have complete trust in their ability to do so under all circumstances.

Although the Zappos Company was only recently formed, its practices are a world-class model for generating employee engagement and mastery. According to Alfred Lin, a former company chairman,

> Zappos was built on the simple premise that to have happy customers, we need happy employees. To have happy employees, we need a great company culture. The success of Zappos demonstrates the linkage between company culture and employee engagement to company success. Our motto of 'Deliver Happiness' for customers and employees was also good for our business and investors.

According to the company website, it implements six strategies to build engagement and mastery:

1. Coworker Bonus Program – this program allows employees to award an extra $50 to a coworker each month for really WOWing their socks off
2. Grant-a-Wish Program – this program allows employees to submit and grant wishes such as sponsoring a citizenship program for an employee who wanted to become an American citizen
3. Zappos $$$ - Zollars are a form of money that can be used only to purchase items from the internal Zollar Store, and are earned when a co-worker feels that an employee has gone above and beyond to serve customers and needs recognition for a job well done
4. Shadow Sessions – an employee can follow another employee in a different department to understand what they do on a daily basis. This builds both company understanding and working relationships.
5. New Hire Scavenger Hunt – After a month-long new hire training, employees are given the names of other employees throughout the company and are challenged to find them and learn what they do
6. Apprenticeships – since most of Zappos' promoting and hiring is done within the company, this program encourages growth and exploration of new career paths

As a result of these efforts, the company has achieved better than a 90% positive customer rating in survey after survey. The company efforts to promote mastery and engagement have not only grown revenue while increasing employee satisfaction and retention, but have also built its reputation as an outstanding customer service company that also sells shoes.

The Principles of Mastery
1. Hire the best in terms of attitude, education, experience, and skills
2. Make employees the first priority in decisions
3. Build employee loyalty, trust, engagement, and commitment
4. Define a structured career progression
5. Actively socialize employees in the core values, credo, and mission
6. Extensively develop employee knowledge, skills, and abilities through education and training

Table 13. The Principles of Mastery

Mastery at Keiunkan

Keiunkan's achievement of mastery is evident from the quiet professionalism exhibited by employees from the moment one sets foot on the property until one leaves, and throughout the entire experience of being at the inn. Yuji admits that hiring for the inn is difficult, and due to its remote location there is a limited pool of candidates from which to choose. He chooses carefully, looking for people who have a natural affinity to the mountains and the natural world in general. With these core values as the base, he builds an expanded awareness of cultural traditions and operational knowledge of the inn. He is acutely aware the employee satisfaction drives customer satisfaction, and this awareness colors his attitudes towards employees.

As has been discussed previously, employees are kept on the payroll during the slow seasons and when disasters such as rockfalls or avalanches occur. During these times, people are assigned other duties as necessary to support the goals of employee retention and loyalty. Since employees undergo extensive socialization processes in cultural traditions and significant on-the-job training efforts, these goals make sense. Keiunkan invests heavily in its employees, which takes considerable time and effort. Once an employee internalizes the core values and attitudes of the inn, they become critical for operational success, and are essential if the inn is to deliver on its brand value promise.

An interesting aspect of the inn is due to its longevity. The bathing practices at the inn have become the model for other inns throughout Japan, and are in and of themselves an established cultural tradition. Over the centuries as the reputation of the inn grew, other ryokans followed the inn's practices and eventually the methods became widespread throughout the country. Employees are aware of this tradition, and Yuji encourages them to feel a strong sense of pride in being able to support it.

Figure 14. The Thousand Year Model

CHAPTER 5

Becoming a Thousand Year Company

One of the most difficult tasks in the day-to-day life of organizational managers is balancing the different priorities of a company. Making a manager's life even more difficult at many companies is the rate at which these priorities can change. In a lot of companies, it is simply not possible to remain focused on sustainability, as priorities can change weekly, daily, or in some cases even hourly. As most managers know, running a company requires continually aligning different systems and processes.

In any company, if it is to be successful, a core priority must be established and reinforced. For a sustainable business, the core priority is survival. In other words, the commitment to survival equates to a commitment to sustainability. A sustainable company is dedicated to doing what is necessary to make sure that operations continue over time. Other considerations, such as growth, money, and power are secondary and are used in service of survival. Short-term expediency is not allowed to become an operating priority, as managers realize that a continued focus on short-term actions will result in long-term damage to the company and threaten its survival.

Sustainable company managers are aware that a company cannot survive if it pollutes the ecosystems on which it depends for its resources, or sickens workers and communities. These managers are also aware that a company cannot survive if it creates a toxic culture that causes employees to leave at the first opportunity, or if employees fail to learn and keep current with the latest technologies, or if it costs more to run the company than it takes in as revenues. Indeed, sustainable company managers acknowledge that only a well-run organization will survive.

Effective sustainability leadership, however, requires going beyond mere operational excellence. Leaders must be creative and offer innovative customer solutions tailored specifically to the capabilities of their companies, and develop meaningful long-term strategies based on their in-depth operational knowledge. The goal is to generate sustainable value for not only customers but for all stakeholders. Every company's position in their markets, communities, and society is unique. Sustainability leaders acknowledge that uniqueness while encouraging managers to take actions to reinforce the relationships necessary to maintain a stable existence over time. As part of a delicate balancing act, these relationship building activities are essentially creative responses to the challenges of change. Bottom line: sustainability leadership is as much an art as it is a science.

In order for any company to function successfully, both leadership and management are required. It is no different for a sustainable company. Leaders define the path forward, while managers act to resolve seemingly conflicting opposites by balancing available resources with organizational goals. The Thousand Year Model reflects the reality that both leadership and management are different, mutually reinforcing, and complementary organizational elements that are absolutely required to keep a company going successfully. Managers develop solutions, remove obstacles, and provide orderly processes, while leaders align the different areas towards a common purpose and motivate people to achieve the company's mission, vision, and values.

At their core, all sustainable companies share a common vision: living together well and flourishing. Each company moves toward this vision through financial gain and building better relationships with people and the natural environment. Flourishing means economic, social, technological, and ecological thriving. The implication is that a sustainable business should make positive contributions that support the integrity, beauty, and stability of our planet and its living inhabitants.

Living together well and flourishing also means that the company seeks financial gain to support its operations. The economic goal is to remain a viable business entity that is able to fulfill a unique core purpose tied to human needs and ecological realities. Sustainable companies seek financial gain not for its own sake, but as a means to achieve its vision of living together well and flourishing.

Living together well also means enabling the world to meets its needs while helping the members of the organization to meet theirs. The business results, i.e. profits and revenues, will come about as a result of fulfilling this purpose, not the other way around. Operational efficiency and the resulting profits are important as they support the continuing existence of the company. Profit, however, is not a goal in and of itself – it is the outcome of providing value for customers and a lagging indicator of success.

In addition, in a sustainable company leaders will eschew growth as a primary goal. They will place emphasis instead on achieving the right operational size based on their specific technology, customer niche, geographic location, and skill base. The awareness is that endless growth within a finite ecosystem is simply not possible, and that at some point organizational complexity will exceed the capabilities of even the best managers. The goal is to optimize the size of the company for adaptability, value provision, and longevity.

Finally, sustainable company leaders will focus on high quality service to customers that generates both short-term satisfaction and long-term loyalty. Rather than seeking to continually increase market share, emphasis is placed on the nature of the customer experience. The goal here, similar to an appropriate size for the business, is an appropriate market share of loyal customers that are delighted with the company's products and services and provide repeat business. Thus, we see that a sustainable company turns traditional business models upside down by pursuing a combination of operational excellence, value creation, and stakeholder relationship quality as drivers of profits. The traditional business model inversion is shown in Figure 21.

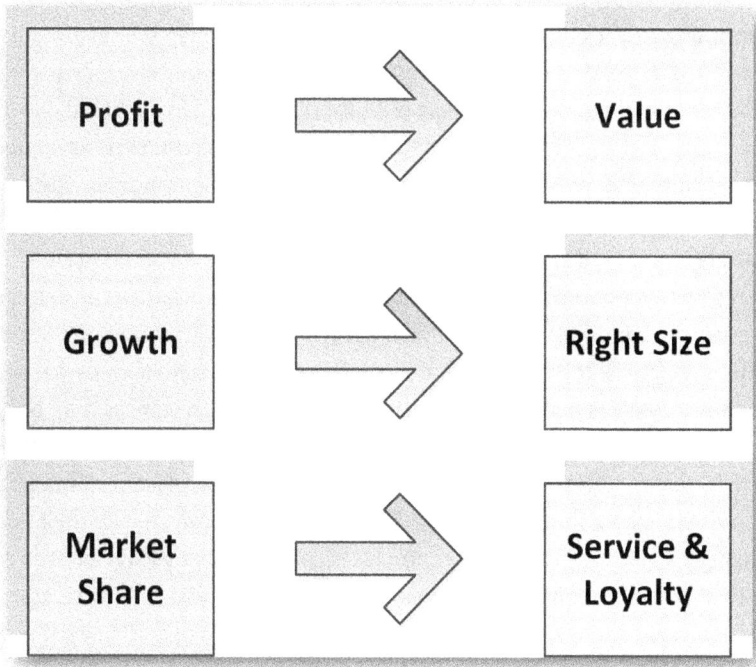

Figure 15. Business Model Inversion

Implementing Sustainable Operations

As with any journey that involves considerable time and expense, experienced travelers want to know where they are going, what is involved in getting there, and why they are taking the journey in the first place. Arguably, the most important part of any journey is not necessarily the destination, but the point of origin, as it determines the path that needs to be taken to arrive at the destination. The important point here is the journey towards becoming a sustainable company will be different for every company because their starting point is different.

Step 1: Recognize your worldview

The first step in becoming a sustainable business involves the internal states of business leaders and hinges on their understanding of what is truly important in order for their companies to remain viable over time. These elements of concern for any sustainable business are defined in The Thousand Year Model. However, before these elements can be addressed business leaders must acknowledge that their beliefs and values align with the purpose and goals of running a sustainable business.

According to ancient Toltec belief, each of us is a dreamer. We dream our world into existence based on what we believe to be true about ourselves, or society, and our environment. We go forth to create what we think is right for us based on what we have been told and what we have learned from others. Since most of us never question the assumptions underlying our dream, most of us live an unquestioning existence. We take others' truths at face value and then believe them so strongly that we seek to experience these truths in all aspects of our lives. We become who we think we are, choosing to live in a world of our own making, and living within the limits of our beliefs and values. We see, hear, and feel what we think is out there in the world, and oftentimes that is not what is actually there, but what our minds tell us to believe about what is there.

Each successive generation lives in different social circumstances than the previous one. When social and ecological conditions are stable, the values and beliefs of succeeding generations will be highly similar. Once formed, a person's core values and beliefs are very stable throughout their lifetime. A person can change their core values and beliefs after the socialization process is complete, but usually does so only in response to a significant life event such as a death, birth, marriage, divorce, trauma, or a crisis. Significant change can emerge as a result of new models and new social behaviors but is realized only through change between successive generations.

In the years preceding and at the beginning of the Industrial Revolution in the 1700's, social conditions were fairly stable. Each successive generation did not significantly challenge the previous generation's behaviors, values, or role models. For some centuries, social structures were unchanging, and a baker's son was highly likely to adopt the trade of being a baker, which in turn would be passed on to his son. The values of successive generations were more similar to those of previous generations than they were different.

In contrast, within the time span of the Industrial Revolution of the past 250 years, societies around the world have begun to destabilize as new technologies, higher levels of education, and rising economic prosperity have created new behaviors never before imaginable. To a person living in 1800, it would have seemed impossible that within the space of single day a person could be on the other side of the world. Such a journey back then took many months to complete, and many people did not even survive the first leg of the voyage. Today we can board a plane and in less than a day be on the opposite side of the Earth from where we started.

A worldview is a person's mental model of the world they inhabit. It is a frame within which existence becomes meaningful based on certain values, beliefs, and attitudes. A worldview defines the means for practical actions and decisions, and is the context within which a person sets their direction in life. A worldview allows a person to determine what is good and evil, right and wrong, and desirable and undesirable. A worldview allows a person to interpret the events around them and make meaning out of a series of inherently meaningless actions.

As human behaviors have changed due to the changing social conditions of the Industrial Revolution, the fundamental values of industrialized societies have remained centered on the mechanistic, Newtonian-Cartesian worldview. This worldview has at its core the commitment to industrial progress as the ultimate purpose of human life, and posits the world as a giant machine that can be manipulated by mechanical means. This commitment is called into question when one begins to ponder what it actually takes to build a sustainable business, and that the world may not actually be a giant machine after all.

This machine-based worldview underpins the vision of industrial progress that has driven societies throughout the world. When combined with the Judeo-Christian tradition of humans dominating the Earth, being cast out of the garden, and being separate from nature, the core assumptions that guide business managers form a powerful worldview that is simply out of date with current reality.

The Limitations of Free Market Philosophy

From an economic viewpoint, many of the assumptions that we use to run our companies today arose primarily from the writings of Adam Smith. Smith was a professor of moral philosophy at the University of Glasgow in the early 1750s. His most famous work, *An Inquiry into the Nature and Causes of the Wealth of Nations*, put forth the central ideas of laissez-faire capitalism that have been the basis of business and economic values for the past 260 years. The essence of this philosophy is the actions of what Smith called the "invisible hand." Here, he presents this idea as part of how an economy should be structured:

> It is not from the benevolence of the butcher, the brewer, or the baker, that we expect our dinner, but from their regard to their own interest. We address ourselves, not to their humanity but to their self-love, and never talk to them of our own necessities but of their advantages...
>
> As every individual who employs his capital in the support of domestic industry, necessarily endeavors so to direct that industry, that its produce may be of the greatest possible value...every individual necessarily labours to render the annual revenue of the society as great as he can. He generally, indeed, neither intends to promote the public interest, nor knows how much he is promoting it. By preferring the support of domestic to that of foreign industry, he intends only his own security; and by directing that industry in such a manner as its produce may be of the greatest value, he intends only his own gain, and he is in this, as in many other cases, led by an invisible hand to promote an end which was no part of his intentions. Nor is it always the worse for the society that it was no part of it. By pursuing his own interest he frequently promotes that of the society more effectually than when he really intends to promote it.

This passage underlies the competitive assumptions of markets and business organizations that have survived to the present day. This approach forms the basis of the free market philosophy which guides the conservative ideals of business throughout the world. Smith also defined what he termed the "natural order of growth" by which every nation should proceed continually: "first agriculture, then manufactures, and finally foreign commerce." Continual economic growth has today become both the unquestioned core assumption and the central goal of economists and many business leaders worldwide.

Unfortunately, another major earlier work by Adam Smith and one that he himself considered superior, *The Theory of Moral Sentiments*, has been largely overlooked. We have misread Smith's laissez-faire approach and as a consequence have developed an unbalanced form of capitalism and business. In *The Theory of Moral Sentiments*, Smith defined an enlightened self-interest, in which moral judgments about others tempered unfettered pursuit of personal gain. Smith established that sympathy for another's plight was the essence of moral judgment and right action, whether the other be rich or poor.

And hence it is, that to feel much for others and little for ourselves, that to restrain our selfish, and to indulge our benevolent affections, constitutes the perfection of human nature; and can alone produce among mankind that harmony of sentiments and passions in which consists their whole grade and propriety. As to love our neighbor as we love ourselves is the great law of Christianity, so it is the great precept of nature to love ourselves only as we love our neighbor, or what comes to the same thing, as our neighbor is capable of loving us…Who does not abhor excessive malice, excessive selfishness, or excessive resentment?…There is something pleasing even in mere instinctive good-will which goes on to do good offices without once reflecting whether by this conduct it is the proper object of either blame or approbation.

Smith goes on to define the proper place of man in society, and in so doing provides the philosophical basis for the essence of sustainability.

Man, according to the Stoics, ought to regard himself, not as something separated and detached, but as a citizen of the world, a member of the vast commonwealth of nature. To the interest of this great community, he ought at all times to be willing that his own little interest should be sacrificed. Whatever concerns himself, ought to affect him no more than whatever concerns any other equally important part of this immense system.

Smith actually defines the principle of compassion by which self-interest should be balanced with concern for others.

Our sensibility to the feelings of others, so far from being inconsistent with the manhood of self-command, is the very principle upon which that manhood is founded. The very same principle or instinct which, in the misfortune of our neighbor, prompts us to compassionate his sorrow; in our own misfortune, prompts us to restrain the abject and miserable lamentations of our own sorrow...The man of most perfect virtue, the man whom we naturally love and revere the most, is he who joins, to the most perfect command of his own original and selfish feelings, the most exquisite sensibility both to the original and sympathetic feelings of others...The man who feels the most for joys and sorrows of others, is best fitted for acquiring the most complete control of his own joys and sorrows.

Smith's essential contribution to the business world was not merely a vision of free market capitalism, but a capitalism tempered by moral restraint. Smith acknowledged the primacy of self-interest as an essential means to survival and core source of motivation. At the same time, he also acknowledged that ethics is a means for keeping excessive self-interest in check in order to accomplish a greater good for society. He saw that a society that allowed free choice of occupation and let each person pursue the form of business that best suited them must maintain itself through moral restraint and dedication to the ideals of benevolence, sympathy, and compassion. People had a duty to pursue moral virtues to prevent their baser nature from taking over, which would unleash their destructive tendencies and damage society.

Perhaps the greatest misfortunes that have befallen many businesses in capitalist societies in the last several hundred years is that they have forgotten the wisdom and moral precepts of *The Theory of Moral Sentiments*, and have lost their foundation of moral restraint. The assumptions of the free market first proposed by Adam Smith have been taken out of the total context of his writings, have gone unquestioned since they were first promulgated, and have been regarded as if they were the sum total of all that is needed in a capitalist society. Business has taken on a distorted version of Smith's vision for capitalism, and many people have used this distorted vision to enrich themselves at the expense of other people and the natural environment. It is the unquestioning adoption of these free market assumptions without their tempering moral precepts that has characterized many business leaders in the Industrial Age and after.

The Emerging Sustainable Worldview

For those leaders and managers seeking sustainability, initially this journey requires a shift in awareness, an acknowledgement of a different dream that requires tempering the destructive tenets of free-market industrialism with compassion and benevolence while moving towards better integration with the living world that supports us. Such a dream is a new frontier to be entered into with respect, reverence, and awe.

Even now, new stories are beginning to be told that transcend the old limited industrial model. We can take inspiration from the very old companies, whose leaders define their organizations as treasures to be guarded, preserved, and sustained for generations yet to come. When we can conceive of a business as a vehicle for making positive contributions for all as well as a means of survival for both human and non-human life, then we will stand upon a new threshold of promise, one in which we embrace the living world in all of its fullness while remaining true to our innermost selves and communities in which we live.

Step 2: Create shared context

As the Earth's climate changes, business leaders are becoming more aware of both the impacts we humans are having on the planet as well as the limitations of the neoclassical business worldview. As a result, the pressures are increasing for a new and different form of commerce to emerge. Business leaders must move away from the destructive tenets of the neoclassical view of the business enterprise, and move towards a more sustainable approach if both humans and the rest of life on the planet are to survive.

As part of this movement, leaders and managers should generate a set of meaningful and compelling ideals to energize followers. Leaders can use the following four general themes as a framework for their visions. These themes outline the essence of our problem and of our solution, and correspond to the four forms of capital we have discussed earlier: economic, social, ecological, and technological.

By considering each theme and its applicability to their company's operations carefully, leaders can establish a sense of meaning and purpose for their company's sustainability journey. Within each of these themes are approaches for treating each specific form of capital in both the neoclassical frame and in the sustainable frame, and a basic path for moving forward. By becoming aware of the frame in which a company is operating and using this awareness to create a shared set of beliefs and values, the leadership can better establish the meaningfulness of its journey to becoming more sustainable.

Theme #1

First, in the economic realm, our theme is to *move away from market efficiency and quantitative growth*. According to David Korten, when markets are freed from restraints and allowed to pursue efficiency as a primary goal, then the results have included (a) individual instead of social advancement, (b) externalization of costs onto the poor and unborn future generations, (c) promotion of consumption that exceeds the capacities of available ecosystem services, and (d) concentration of wealth and the concomitant reduction of income equality. Quantitative growth assumes infinite substitution of human capital for natural capital, as well as infinite growth within a finite and closed world ecosystem. These assumptions are simply not realistic given the degraded ecological conditions of today's world and our understanding of the limitations of technology.

Therefore, in order to solve these problems our economic theme is to *move towards fostering social justice and qualitative development*. This means that the company leaders will promote public accountability for their company's actions as well as the actions of other companies, support people leading fulfilling lives and achieving their potential, and provide prices that reflect social and ecological costs. Moving towards this outcome implies support for reducing the primacy of consumption as a social goal and instead raising the importance of nonmaterial sources of happiness such as family and community relationships, leisure time well spent, and meaningful employment.

Theme #2

In the social realm, our theme is to *move away from atomism and individualism*. The important point here is that a functioning society is much more than a collection of individuals motivated by rational self-interest and greed; it is an organized set of communities that are all interrelated in a number of different ways. Individuals are not merely autonomous units existing independently of government, society, and the natural world, but are members of communities in which they can fulfill their roles as public citizens working together for the common good.

Sustainable companies will seek to strengthen the communities of which they are a part, including their internal community of employees. They will also instill in their customers a sense of restraint for purchasing the company's products and services based on needs, not wants. People are motivated in different ways and thrive under very different cultures, yet the public good is one characteristic that all societies share.

Thus, in order to solve these problems, our social theme is to *move towards social integrity and holism.*

Theme #3

Within in the ecological realm, our theme is to *move away from anthropocentrism and rationalism.* The value of ecosystem services and the ecosystems themselves cannot always be reduced to only economic terms or forced to fit within a mathematical equation. There are moral and aesthetic considerations such as beauty and goodness that simply cannot be defined quantitatively nor be evaluated by positivist means. In addition, human beings are not the only species that inhabits the planet – we just act like it. We have been conquerors of nature through the use of science, oftentimes with disastrous results such as ecosystem destruction, species extinction, and climate change. Nature has been viewed as a giant set of resources to be exploited for human gain while ignoring the effects on the world's living systems, and this notion is simply not sustainable.

In order to solve these problems, our ecological theme is to *move towards biocentrism and intuitionism,* where humans are one species among many and our world is valued in many ways, including as a life support system for now and for unborn generations for all time. Sustainable company leadership will emphasize the company's role as a steward of the natural world, and promote both quantitative and qualitative valuations of the ecosystems that it impacts with its operations.

Theme #4

Finally, in the technological realm, our theme is to move *away from techno-optimism and proximity.* Every technology is a two-edged sword with both benefits and detriments, and many of the negative impacts of a specific technology do not become visible until after the technology has been fully disseminated throughout society.

Increasing complexity over time is a characteristic of all technological systems, and some social systems as well. Technologies that have been allowed to evolve and become overly complex suffer from exponentially greater times required for maintenance and repair, until in some cases more time is spent fixing the technology and restoring its negative impacts than operating the technology itself. In some cases, such as nuclear power generation, there are multiple issues that can only be observed when viewing the technology from a greater distance in space and time, which means a life cycle perspective. For example, nuclear power appears to be purely beneficial when viewed from a time frame related only to the operation of a plant, but when viewed from a life cycle perspective beginning with the mining of the raw materials and ending with the eventual the storage of spent nuclear fuels and plant decommissioning, this technology introduces problems for which there is no known solution using current technologies.

Therefore, in order to prevent these problems, our technology theme is to *move towards techno-skepticism and distance*, and consider the long-term impacts and life cycles of emerging technologies. The desirable approach is to consider the social and ecological impacts of all emerging technologies beginning with raw material origins and ending with waste disposal. When it seems like an emerging technology is going to negatively impact the beauty, integrity, and stability of the Earth's living systems, then leaders should approach the development of this technology with caution.

Step 3: Begin where you are

An important aspect of The Thousand Year Model is that it does not prescribe a set of activities to be performed in a step-by-step manner. Rather, this model offers a general framework within which a company can situate itself for its sustainability journey. Any entry point is acceptable, and should be based on the current strengths of the organization. The implication is that an honest self-assessment is needed: the leaders must answer the question "What are we good at?" and use the answer as a starting point for the development of the systems and processes that will support the company's sustainable operations.

Moreover, a company does not have excel at all of the elements of The Thousand Year Model to be sustainable. It should, however, address all of the elements to some degree and select an element or elements from which it will derive its distinctive brand value and competitive advantage. The adage that one should "build on one's strengths" is very applicable here. Any company wishing to undertake the journey to sustainable operations must decide not only their starting point, but also where they are going to locate themselves within The Thousand Year Model framework based on the company purpose, technology, location, and employee skills.

The majority of the long-lived companies have selected one or two elements of The Thousand Year Model as the basis for their competitive excellence. These elements are their strengths and are carried down through successive generations. For example, Zildjian uses its skills at manufacturing combined with its aesthetic sensibility to create a musical instrument that cannot be imitated by competitors.

Another example is the Berretta Company, founded in 1526, which fuses its design aesthetic with advanced, proprietary manufacturing methods developed by the company. Craftsmen train for many years to produce weapons that are both works of art and highly functional, and that clearly show the distinctive style of the company. The company describes its philosophy as a commitment "to beauty, to craftsmanship, to passion, and to the pursuit of perfection." The Berretta specialty firearms products reflect this philosophy in their fusion of aesthetic elegance and refinement, function, and high performance in products designed to last for many years.

A different example is the Shirley Plantation in Virginia, USA, which was founded in 1613. The plantation's primary forms of business are tourism and leasing farmland, and it is both an active farm as well as an historic landmark. The company's competitive advantage comes from its stakeholder integration and brand integrity: tourists of all ages come and visit the main buildings, which are a National Historic Landmark. The company hosts meetings and events of all types for both the public as well as other private businesses, and the income from leased farmlands helps to sustain the economic dimension of plantation life.

The point here is that there is no one right way to achieve sustainability. Every company must define why it exists and then how it is going to sustain itself to achieve that purpose over time. Sustainability will look very different in different organizations: there is no silver bullet or one size fits all. Rather, it is through the work of continually defining itself and creating meaningful customer experiences that a business will make its way down the path towards sustainable operations.

Beginning the journey is, however, one aspect of building a sustainable company that all organizations will share. They should start with their strengths, and define for themselves how they can build on these strengths over time. The entry point to the path towards sustainable operations is simply where you are now.

Epilogue

The world today is continuing to change, yet much remains the same. Human needs are growing along with the expanding population, while the conditions necessary for the survival of both human and non-human life are being eroded daily. The role of business, as a social institution consuming resources and generating wastes, is a major contributor to the changes in the Earth's ecosystems. These changes can affect the ability of the planet to support life, and can directly impact the survival of both humans and other living species. Business leaders can choose whether their impacts are positive or negative, whether they destroy or restore our life support systems, and whether their company prospers or collapses.

At its core, the business leadership approach found in The Thousand Year Model consists of only several simple ideas. These ideas are that a business should:

- Develop processes and structures that ensure its continuity through time
- Support the continued existence of its members, their communities, human civilization, and the rest of life on Earth
- Help its members and stakeholders to thrive and flourish

When business leaders align their companies with our innermost needs as human beings, a new path into the future opens up. Although this path is each leader's alone to take, they will take it with the certain knowledge that it is the right thing to do and that many others have walked this path before them.

Life is change and motion. Moving an organization towards survival, thriving, and mutual prosperity means that leaders will have no choice but to ride the waves of change and move forward in their organizations and in society. As companies travel along this path, the core leadership challenges become clear: imbuing the organization with the values and significance of the founder's vision, fanning the flames of the burning fires that drive human activities, and linking organizational actions to the highest good for humanity and for all forms of living beings on the planet.

Business leaders do not have to make this journey alone. There are hundreds of examples of companies that have sustained themselves over the centuries, passing along wisdom that is readily available. It is my hope that you take advantage of this wisdom, some of which is captured in this book, and make it yours as you journey onwards.

Figure 16. The path to the future

Further Readings and References

Anderson, R. C. (1998). *Mid-course correction: Toward a sustainable enterprise: the Interface model.* White River Junction, VT: Chelsea Green Publishing Company.

Anderson, R. C. (2003). Toward and just and sustainable economy: Economics 101 revisited. *Corporate Environmental Strategy, 10*(6), 4-27-4-32.

Anderson, R. C. (2010). *Business lessons from a radical industrialist.* New York, NY: St. Martin's Press.

Aoki, K., & Lennerfors, T. T. (2013). The new, improved keiretsu. *Harvard Business Review, 91*(9), 109-113.

Argyris, C. (1976). *Increasing leadership effectiveness.* New York, NY: John Wiley & Sons, Inc.

Audebrand, L. K. (2010). Sustainability in strategic management education: the quest for new root metaphors. *Academy of Management Learning & Education, 9*(3), 413-428.

Aurobindo, S. (1990). *The future evolution of man: The divine life upon earth.* Twin Lakes, WI: Lotus Press.

Bansal, P. (2005). Evolving sustainably: A longitudinal study of corporate sustainable development. *Strategic Management Journal, 26,* 197-218.

Bates, T. (1990). Entrepreneur human capital inputs and small business longevity. *The Review of Economics and Statistics, 72*(4), 551-559.

Bazerman, M. H., Messick, D. M., Tenbrunsel, A. E., & Wade-Benzoni, K. A. (Eds.). (1997). *Environment, ethics, and behavior.* San Francisco, CA: The New Lexington Press.

Beinhocker, E. D. (2006). The adaptable corporation. *The McKinsey Quarterly, 2,* 77-87. Retrieved from http://www.synetz-international.com/Artikel_Adaptable_corporation_McK.pdf

Bell, M. A. (2002). *The Five Principles Of Organizational Resilience*. Retrieved from https://www.gartner.com/doc/351410/principles-organizational-resilience

Benn, S., Dunphy, D., & Griffiths, A. (2014). *Organizational Change For Corporate Sustainability* (3rd ed.). New York, NY: Routledge.

Bernasek, A. (2010). *The Economics Of Integrity*. New York, NY: HarperStudio.

Berns, M., Townend, A., Khayat, Z., Balagopal, B., Reeves, M., Hopkins, M. S., & Kruschwitz, N. (2009). Sustainability and competitive advantage. *MIT Sloan Management Review, 51*(1), 19-26.

Berns, M., Townend, A., Khayat, Z., Balagopal, B., Reeves, M., Hopkins, M. S., & Kruschwitz, N. (2009). The business of sustainability: What it means to managers now. *MIT Sloan Management Review, 51*(1), 2-12.

Berrone, P., Cruz, C., Gomez-Mejia, L. R., & Larraza-Kintana, M. (2010). Socioemotional wealth and corporate response to institutional pressures: Do family-owned firms pollute less? *Administrative Science Quarterly, 99*, 82-113.

Berry, T. (1988). *The Dream Of The Earth*. San Francisco, CA: Sierra Club Books.

Berry, W. (1983). The specialization of poetry. In *Standing by words: Essays* (pp. 3-23). Berkeley, CA: Counterpoint Press.

Bieker, T., Dyllick, T., Gminder, C. U., & Hockerts, K. (2001). Towards a sustainability balanced scorecard: Linking environmental and social sustainability to business strategy. In *Conference Proceedings of Business Strategy and the Environment*. Geneva, Switzerland: University of St. Gallen.

Bingham, J. B., Dyer, W. G., Smith, I., & Adams, G. L. (2011). A stakeholder identity orientation approach to corporate social performance. *Journal of Business Ethics, 99*, 565-585.

Birkinshaw, J., Foss, N. J., & Lindenberg, S. (2014). Combining purpose with profits. *MIT Sloan Management Review, 55*(3), 49-56.

Blake, R. R., Avis, W. E., & Mouton, J. S. (1966). *Corporate Darwinism*. Houston, TX: Gulf Publishing.

Boisot, M. H. (1995). Is your firm a creative destroyer? Competitive learning and knowledge flows in the technological strategies of firms. *Research Policy, 24*, 489-506.

Brand, S. (1999). *The clock of the long now: Time and responsibility*. New York, NY: Basic Books.

Bruderl, J., & Preisendorfer, P. (1992). Survival chances of newly founded business organizations. *American Sociological Review, 57*, 227-242.

Cahn, S. M., & Meskin, A. (Eds.). (2008). *Aesthetics: A comprehensive anthology.* Malden, MA: Blackwell Publishing.

Capra, F. (1987). *The Turning Point: Science, Society, And The Rising Culture.* New York, NY: Simon & Schuster.

Chartered Institute of Management Accountants, Canadian Institute of Chartered Accountants, & American Institute of Certified Public Accountants. (2011). *SMEs set their sights on sustainability: Case studies of small and medium-sized enterprises (SMEs) from the UK, US, and Canada.* Retrieved from http://www.aicpa.org/interestareas/ businessindustryandgovernment/resources/sustainability/downloadabledocuments/ sustainability_case_studies_final%20pdf.pdf

Chouinard, Y., Ellison, J., & Ridgeway, R. (2011). The sustainable economy. *Harvard Business Review, 89*(10), 52-62.

Chouinard, Y., & Stanley, V. (2012). *The Responsible Company: What We've Learned From Patagonia's First 40 Years.* Ventura, CA: Patagonia Books.

Clegg, S., Courpasson, D., & Phillips, N. (2006). *Power and organizations.* Thousand Oaks, CA: SAGE Publications Inc.

Cropp, R. C., & Gabric, A. (n.d.). Ecosystem adaptation: Do ecosystems maximize resilience? *Ecology and Society.*

Cropp, R., & Gabric, A. (2002). Ecosystem adaptation: Do ecosystems maximize resilience? *Ecology, 83*(7), 2019-2026.

Cross, R., Gray, P., Cunningham, S., Showers, M., & Thomas, R. J. (2010). The collaborative organization: How to make employee networks really work. *MIT Sloan Management Review, 52*(1), 83-90.

Cutts, R. L. (1992). Capitalism in Japan: Cartels and keiretsu. *Harvard Business Review, 70*(4), 48-55.

Dapkus, M. A. (1985). A thematic analysis of the experience of time. *Journal of Personality and Social Psychology, 49*(2), 408-419.

Davis, E. W. (2004). *The Extended Enterprise: Gaining Competitive Advantage Through Collaborative Supply Chains.* Upper Saddle River, NJ: Financial Times Prentice-Hall.

De Geus, A. (2002). *The Living Company: Habits For Survival In A Turbulent Business Environment.* Boston, MA: Harvard Business Review Press.

De Groot, R. S., Wilson, M. A., & Boumans, R. M. (2002). A typology for the classification, description and valuation of ecosystem functions, goods and services. *Ecological Economics, 41*, 393-408.

Dean, J. W., Ottensmeyer, E., & Ramirez, R. (1997). An aesthetic perspective on organizations. In C. L. Cooper & S. E. Jackson (Eds.), *Creating tomorrow's organizations: A handbook for future research in organizational behavior.* New York, NY: John Wiley.

Deloitte. (2013, April 26). *Culture of Purpose: A business imperative: 2013 core beliefs & culture survey.* Retrieved from http://www.deloitte.com/view/en_US/us/About/Leadership/3b7a33d2eacae310VgnVCM1000003256f70aRCRD.htm

Domhoff, G. W. (2005, April). *Basics of studying power.* Retrieved from http://www2.ucsc.edu/whorulesamerica/methods/studying_power.html

Doppelt, B. (2008). *The Power Of Sustainable Thinking.* Sterling, VA: Earthscan.

Drucker, P. F. (1994). The theory of the business. *Harvard Business Review, 72*(5), 95-104.

Drucker, P. F. (2002). They're not employees, they're people. *Harvard Business Review, 80*(2), 70-77.

Drucker, P. F. (2004). What makes an effective executive. *Harvard Business Review, 82*(6), 61-72.

Du Nann Winter, D., & Koger, S. M. (2004). *The Psychology Of Environmental Problems* (2nd ed.). Mahwah, NJ: Lawrence Earlbaum Associates.

Duke, D. L. (1986). The aesthetics of leadership. *Educational Administration Quarterly, 22*(1), 7-27.

Duncan, R. C. (1993). The life-expectancy of industrial civilization: the decline to global equilibrium. *Population and Environment, 14*(4), 325-357.

Dyer, J. H. (1996). How Chrysler created an American keiretsu. *Harvard Business Review, 74*(4), 42-56.

Eccles, R. G., Perkins, K. M., & Serafeim, G. (2012). How to become a sustainable company. *MIT Sloan Management Review, 53*(4), 43-50.

The Economist. (2004, December 16). *The business of survival.* Retrieved from http://www.economist.com/node/3490684

Ehrenfeld, J. R. (2005). The roots of sustainability. *MIT Sloan Management Review, 46*(2), 23-25.

Elgin, D. (2000). *Promise Ahead: A Vision Of Hope And Action For Humanity's Future.* New York, NY: HarperCollins Books.

Engleman, R. (2014). Beyond sustainababble. In L. Brown (Ed.), *State of the world 2013* (pp. 3-18). Washington, DC: Island Press.

Figge, F., Hahn, T., Schaltegger, S., & Wagner, M. (2002). The sustainability balanced scorecard: Linking sustainability management to business strategy. *Business Strategy and the Environment, 11*, 269-284.

Folke, C., Carpenter, S. R., Walker, B., Scheffer, M., Chapin, T., & Rockstrom, J. (2010). Resilience thinking: Integrating resilience, adaptability, and transformability. *Ecology and Society, 15*(4), 20-29.

Ford, P. (2009, July 19). What is aesthetics? [Web log post]. Retrieved from http://paulford.com/what-is-aesthetics/

Franken, R. E. (2007). *Human motivation* (6th ed.). Belmont, CA: Thomson Wadsworth.

Freeman, R. E., Harrison, J. S., & Wicks, A. C. (2007). *Managing for stakeholders: Survival, reputation, and success.* New Haven, CT: Yale University Press.

Freeman, R. E., Harrison, J. S., Wicks, A. C., Parmar, B. L., & De Colle, S. (2010). *Stakeholder Theory: The state of the art.* New York, NY: Cambridge University Press.

Friedman, A. L., & Miles, S. (2006). *Stakeholders: Theory and practice.* Oxford, UK: Oxford University Press.

Fryer, B. (2001). High tech the old-fashioned way. *Harvard Business Review, 79*(3), 118-125.

Garvin, D. A., Edmondson, A. C., & Gino, F. (2008). Is yours a learning organization? *Harvard Business Review, 86*(3), 109-116.

Gibbs, T., Heywood, S., & Pettigrew, M. (2012). Encouraging your people to take the long view. *McKinsey Quarterly, , .* Retrieved from http://www.mckinsey.com/insights/organization/encouraging_your_people_to_take_the_long_view

Gittleson, K. (2012, June 6). *Trade secrets of oldest family firm in US.* Retrieved from http://www.bbc.com/news/business-18261045

Gladwin, T. N., Kennelly, J. J., & Krause, T. S. (1995). Shifting paradigms for sustainable development: Implications for management theory and research. *Academy of Management Review, 20*(4), 874-907.

Gomory, R., & Sylla, R. (2013). The American corporation. *Daedalus, the Journal of the American Academy of Arts & Sciences, 142*(2), 102-118.

Graf, P. (2010). How SAP made the business case for sustainability. *MIT Sloan Management Review, 51*(4), 2-6.

Grant, A. (2013). *Give And Take: Why Helping Others Drives Our Success.* New York, NY: Penguin Books.

Greer, J. M. (2005). *How Civilizations Fall: A Theory Of Catabolic Collapse.* Retrieved from http://www.ecoshock.org/transcripts/greer_on_collapse.pdf

Greer, J. M. (2008). *The Long Descent: A User's Guide To The End Of The Industrial Age.* Gabriola Island BC, Canada: New Society Publishers.

Greer, J. M. (2012). *Mystery Teachings From The Living Earth: An Introduction To Spiritual Ecology*. San Francisco, CA: Weiser Books.

Greiner, L. E. (1998). Evolution and revolution as organizations grow. *Harvard Business Review, 76*(3), 55-67.

Griffiths, A., & Petrick, J. A. (2001). Corporate architectures for sustainability. *International Journal of Operations & Production Management, 21*(12), 1573-1585.

Gunderson, L. H. (2000). Ecological resilience in theory and application. *Annual Review of Ecological systems, 31*, 425-439.

Haanaes, K., Arthur, D., Balagopal, B., Teck Kong, M., Reeves, M., Velken, I.,... Kruschwitz, N. (2011, November/December). *Sustainability: The 'embracers' seize advantage*. Retrieved from http://sloanreview.mit.edu/reports/sustainability-advantage/

Haanaes, K., Michael, D., Jurgens, J., & Rangan, S. (2013). Making sustainability profitable. *Harvard Business Review, 91*(7), 110-114.

Haanaes, K., Reeves, M., Streng Velken, I., Audretsch, M., Kiron, D., & Kruschwitz, N. (2012). Sustainability nears a tipping point. *MIT Sloan Management Review, 53*(2), 69-94.

Hansen, H., Ropo, A., & Sauer, E. (2007). Aesthetic leadership. *The Leadership Quarterly, 18*, 544-560.

Hanson, C., Van Der Lugt, C., & Ozment, S. (2011). *Nature in performance: Initial recommendations for integrating ecosystem services into business performance systems.* Retrieved from http://www.wri.org/sites/default/files/pdf/nature_in_performance.pdf

Hart, S. L. (1995). A natural-resource-based view of the firm. *Academy of Management Review, 20*(4), 986-1014.

Hart, S. L., & Milstein, M. B. (1999). Global sustainability and the creative destruction of industries. *MIT Sloan Management Review, 41*(1), 23-32.

Hart, S. L., & Milstein, M. B. (2003). Creating sustainable value. *Academy of Management Executive, 17*(2), 56-69.

Haslam, S. A. (2004). *Psychology In Organizations: The Social Identity Approach.* Thousand Oaks, CA: Sage Publications.

Hawken, P. (1993). *The Ecology Of Commerce: A Declaration Of Sustainability.* New York, NY: HarperBusiness.

Hawken, P., Lovins, A., & Lovins, L. H. (1999). *Natural Capitalism: Creating The Next Industrial Revolution.* New York, NY: Little, Brown and Company.

Hayek, M. (2013). *Jaquet Droz: Swiss watchmaker since 1738.* Geneva, Switzerland: Jaquet Droz.

Hayes, F. (2005, April 18). Death of a salesman. *ComputerWorld*.

Headd, B. (2003). Redefining business success: Distinguishing between closure and failure. *Small Business Economics, 21*, 51-61.

Headd, B., & Kirchoff, B. (2009). The growth, decline and survival of small businesses: An exploratory study of life cycles. *Journal of Small Business Management, 47*(4), 531-550.

Hekker, P. (2006). Design aesthetics: Principles of pleasure in design. *Psychology Science, 48*(2), 157-172.

Henry, A. D. (2009). The challenge of learning for sustainability: A prolegomenon to theory. *Human Ecology Review, 16*(2), 131-139.

Hillman, J. (1995). *Kinds of Power: A guide to its intelligent uses*. New York, NY: Doubleday.

Hopkins, M. S. (2009). 8 reasons sustainability will change management (that you never thought of). *MIT Sloan Management Review, 51*(1), 27-30.

Hopkins, M. S. (2009). What executives don't get about sustainability (and further notes on the profit motive). *MIT Sloan Management Review, 51*(1), 35-40.

Hosey, L. (2012). *The shape of green*. Washington, DC: Island Press.

Howard, G. S. (1997). *Ecological Psychology: Creating A More Earth-Friendly Human Nature*. Notre Dame, IN: University of Notre Dame Press.

Howard, V. A. (1996). The aesthetic face of leadership. *Journal of Aesthetic Education, 30*(4), 21-37.

Hughes, B. (2013, August 17). *Levi's sews sustainability into brand from ground up*. Retrieved from http://www.sfgate.com/style/article/Levi-s-sews-sustainability-into-brand-from-ground-4738823.php

Iansiti, M., & Levien, R. (2004). Strategy as ecology. *Harvard Business Review, 82*(3), 69-78.

Inglehart, R., & Baker, W. E. (2000). Modernization, cultural change, and the persistence of traditional values. *American Sociological Review, 65*, 19-51.

Iroquois Nation. (2014). *Iroquois constitution*. Retrieved from http://www.indigenouspeople.net/iroqcon.htm

Iwasaki, N., & Kanda, M. (1995). *Sustainability of the Japanese old established companies*. Retrieved from http://www.seijo.ac.jp/pdf/faeco/kenkyu/0003/132-iwasaki-kanda01.pdf

Jackson, T., & Marks, N. (1999). Consumption, sustainable welfare and human needs-with reference to UK expenditure patterns between 1954 and 1994. *Ecological Economics, 28*, 421-441.

Kahn, P. H., & Hasbach, P. H. (Eds.). (2012). *Ecopsychology: Science, totems, and the technological species.* Cambridge, MA: The MIT Press.

Kanda, M. (2013). *Lessons from the Shinise.* Paper presented at the Annual Meeting of the Tokyo Chamber of Commerce. Tokyo, Japan.

Kanda, M. (2014). *Learn from the strengths of the Shinise.* Paper presented at the Annual Meeting of the Tokyo Chamber of Commerce. Tokyo, Japan.

Kane, G. C. (2014, January 10). Which game are you playing? [Web log post]. Retrieved from http://sloanreview.mit.edu/article/which-game-are-you-playing/

Kanter, E. M. (1979). Power failure in management circuits. *Harvard Business Review, 57*(4), 65-75.

Katsuhiko, T. (2010, March 24). *The longevity secret of Kyoto businesses.* Retrieved from http://www.asahi.com/english/TKY201003230325.html

Keijzers, G. (2002). The transition to the sustainable enterprise. *Journal of Cleaner Production, 10,* 349-359.

Kiron, D., Kruschwitz, N., Haanes, K., Reeves, M., & Goh, E. (2013). The innovation bottom line. *MIT Sloan Management Review, 54*(3), 1-20.

Knaup, A. E. (2005, May). *Survival and longevity in the business employment dynamics data.* Retrieved from http://stats.bls.gov/opub/mlr/2005/05/ressum.pdf

Knaup, A. E., & Piazza, M. C. (2007, September). *Business employment dynamics data: Survival and longevity: II.* Retrieved from http://www.bls.gov/opub/mlr/2007/09/art1full.pdf

Koren, L. (1992). *How to take a Japanese bath.* Berkely, CA: Stone Bridge Press.

Koren, L. (2008). *Wabi Sabi for artisits, designers, poets & philosophers.* Point Reyes, CA: Imperfect Publishing.

Koren, L. (2010). *Which "Aesthetics" Do You Mean? Ten Definitions.* Point Reyes, CA: Imperfect Publishing.

Koren, L. (2015). *Wabi Sabi: Further thoughts.* Point Reyes, CA: Imperfect Publishing.

Korten, D. C. (2001). *When Corporations Rule The World.* San Francisco, CA: Berrett-Koehler Publishers, Inc.

Korten, D. C. (2006). *The Great Turning: From Empire To Earth Community.* San Francisco, CA: Berrett-Koehler Publishers, Inc.

Korten, D. C. (2010). *Agenda For A New Economy: From Phantom Wealth To Real Wealth.* San Francisco, CA: Berrett-Koehler Publishers, Inc.

Krantz, M., & Swartz, J. (2011, June 16). IBM joins elite group of 100-year old companies. *USA Today.* Retrieved from http://usatoday30.usatoday.com/money/companies/management/2011-06-15-ibm-corporate-longevity_n.htm

Labuschagne, C., Brent, A. C., & Van Erck, R. P. (2005). Assessing the sustainability performance of industries. *Journal of Cleaner Production, 13,* 373-385.

Lammers, J., Stapel, D. A., & Galinsky, A. D. (2010). Powers increases hypocrisy: Moralizing in reasoning, immorality in behavior. *Psychological Science, 21*(5), 737-744.

Lawler, E. E., & Worley, C. G. (2012). Why boards need to change. *MIT Sloan Management Review, 54*(1), 75-81.

Leonard, T. C. (2009). Origins of the myth of social Darwinism: the ambiguous legacy of Richard Hofstadter's Social Darwinism in American Thought. *Journal of Economic Behavior & Organization, 71,* 37-51.

Levinson, D. J. (1978). *The Seasons Of A Man's Life.* New York, NY: Ballantine Books.

Liker, J. K., & Choi, T. Y. (2004). Building deep supplier relationships. *Harvard Business Review, 82*(12), 104-113.

Lindenberg, S., & Foss, N. J. (2011). Managing joint production motivation: the role of goal framing and governance mechanisms. *Academy of Management Review, 36*(3), 500-525.

Lo, S. F., & Sheu, H. J. (2007). Is corporate sustainability a value-increasing strategy for business? *Corporate Governance, 15*(2), 345-357.

Lubin, D. A., & Esty, D. C. (2010). The sustainability imperative. *Harvard Business Review, 88*(5), 44-50.

Lueneburger, C., & Goleman, D. (2010). The change leadership sustainability demands. *MIT Sloan Management Review, 51*(4), 49-55.

Lukes, S. (Ed.). (1986). *Power.* Washington Squary, NY: The New York University Press.

Lussier, R. N., & Halabi, C. E. (2010). A three-country comparison of the business success versus failure prediction model. *Journal of Small Business Management, 48*(3), 360-377.

Luthans, F., Youssef, C. M., & Avolio, B. J. (2007). *Psychological capital: Developing the human competitive edge.* New York, NY: Oxford University Press.

Mackey, J., & Sisodia, R. (2014). *Conscious Capitalism: Liberating The Heroic Spirit Of Business.* Boston, MA: Harvard Business Review Press.

Makower, J. (2011, August 6). *Why aren't there more Ray Andersons?* Retrieved from http://www.greenbiz.com/blog/2012/08/06/why-aren%E2%80%99t-there-more-ray-andersons

Mannheim, K. (1952). The problem of generations. In P. Kecskemeti (Ed.), *Essays on the sociology of knowledge* (pp. 276-321). New York, NY: Oxford University Press.

Maslow, A. H. (1943). A theory of human motivation. *Psychological Review, 50,* 370-396.

Maslow, A. H. (1998). *Maslow on management*. New York, NY: John Wiley & Sons, Inc.

Massey, M. (1979). *The people puzzle: Understanding yourself and others*. Reston, VA: Reston Publishing Company.

Max-Neef, M. (2014). The good is the bad that we don't do: Economic crimes against humanity: A proposal. *Ecological Economics*. Retrieved from http://dx.doi.org/10.1016/j.ecolecon.2014.02.011

Max-Neef, M. A. (1991). *Human scale development: Conception, application, and further reflections*. New York, NY: Apex Press.

McClelland, D. C., & Burnham, D. H. (2003). Power is the great motivator. *Harvard Business Review, 81*(1), 117-126.

McDonough, W., & Braungart, M. (2002). *Cradle To Cradle: Remaking The Way We Make Things*. New York, NY: North Point Press.

McDonough, W., & Braungart, M. (2013). *The upcycle*. New York, NY: North Point Press.

Means, H. (2001). *Money & power: the history of business*. New York, NY: John Wiley & Sons.

Meyer, C., & Schwager, A. (2007). Understanding customer experience. *Harvard Business Review, 85*(2), 117-126.

Micklethwait, J., & Woolridge, A. (2005). *The Company: A Short History Of A Revolutionary Idea*. New York, NY: The Modern Library.

Miller, D., & Le Breton-Miller, I. (2005). *Managing For The Long Run: Lessons In Competitive Advantage From Great Family Businesses*. Boston, MA: Harvard Business School Press.

Mintzberg, H. (2009). Rebuilding companies as communities. *Harvard Business Review, 87*(7), 140-143.

Montiel, I., & Delgado-Ceballos, J. (2014). Defining and measuring corporate sustainability: Are we there yet? *Organization & Environment, ,* 1-27. doi:10.1177/1086026614526413

Muson, H. (1993, Summer). How to build a dynasty. *Family Business*.

Nidumolu, R., Prahalad, C. K., & Rangaswami, M. R. (2009). Why sustainability is now the key driver of innovation. *Harvard Business Review, 87*(9), 57-64.

Nucci, A. R. (1999). The demography of business closings. *Small Business Economics, 12*, 25-39.

O'Hara, W. T. (2004). *Centuries Of Success: Lessons From The World's Most Enduring Family Businesses*. Avon, MA: Adams Media.

O'Reilly, C. (2013, May 31). *Why some companies seem to last forever*. Retrieved from http://www.gsb.stanford.edu/news/headlines/charles-oreilly-why-some-companies-seem-last-forever

Patrick, M. (2002). The leadership aesthetics of Saint Francis of Assisi. *Inner Resources for Leaders, 1*(2), . Retrieved from http://www.regent.edu/acad/global/publications/innerresources/vol1iss2/patrick_insp_leader.pdf

Perman, S. (2008, May 14). Centuries-old family businesses share their secrets. *Bloomberg BusinessWeek*. Retrieved from http://www.businessweek.com/stories/2008-05-14/centuries-old-family-businesses-share-their-secretsbusinessweek-business-news-stock-market-and-financial-advice

Petri, H. L., & Govern, J. M. (2004). *Motivation: Theory, research, and applications* (5th ed.). Belmont, CA: Thomson Wadsworth.

Pfeffer, J. (1992). Understanding power in organizations. *California Management Review, 34*(2), 29-50.

Pfeffer, J. (2010). Building sustainable organizations: The human factor. *Academy of Management Perspectives, 24*(1), 34-45.

Pfitzer, M., Bockstette, V., & Stamp, M. (2013). Innovating for shared value: Companies that deliver both social benefit and business value rely on five mutually reinforcing elements. *Harvard Business Review, 91*(9), 101-107.

Piaget, J. (1985). *Equilibration of cognitive structures: The central problem of intellectual development (T. Brown and K.J. Thampy, Trans.)*. Chicago, IL: University of Chicago Press.

Port, J. D. (2013). Feeling connected: 7 ways to enhance workplace relationships, motivation, and productivity. *Quality Progress, 43*(7), 17-20.

Porter, M. E., & Kramer, M. R. (2011). Creating shared value: How to reinvent capitalism-and unleash a wave of innovation and growth. *Harvard Business Review, 89*(1/2), 62-77.

Quigley, C. (1970). Our ecological crisis. *Current History, 59*(347), 1-49.

Ramirez, R. (1996). Wrapping form and organizational beauty. *Organization, 3*(2), 233-242.

Rawson, A., Duncan, E., & Jones, C. (2013). The truth about customer experience. *Harvard Business Review, 91*(9), 90-98.

Ready, D. A., & Truelove, E. (2011). The power of collective ambition. *Harvard Business Review, 89*(12), 95-102.

Richie, D. (2007). *A Tractate On Japanese Aesthetics*. Berkely, CA: Stone Bridge Press.

Rigby, D. K., Reichheld, F. F., & Schefter, P. (2002). Avoid the four perils of CRM. *Harvard Business Review, 80*(2), 101-109.

Roszak, T., Gomes, M. E., & Kanner, A. D. (Eds.). (1995). *Ecopsychology: Restoring the earth, healing the mind.* San Francisco, CA: Sierra Club Books.

Sakai, K. (1990). The feudal world of Japanese manufacturing. *Harvard Business Review, 68*(6), 38-49.

Schmuck, P., & Vlek, C. (2003). Psychologists can do much to support sustainable development. *European Psychologist, 8*(2), 66-76.

Schumaker, E. F. (1989). *Small is beautiful.* New York, NY: Harper & Row.

Scruton, R. (2011). *Beauty: A very short introduction.* New York, NY: Oxford University Press.

Sekerka, L. E., & Stimel, D. (2011). How durable is sustainable enterprise? Ecological sustainability meets the reality of tough times. *Business Horizons, 54,* 112-124.

Senge, P. (2009). Sustainability: Not what you think it is. *MIT Sloan Management Review, 50*(4), 2-8.

Shrivastava, P., & Hart, S. (1995). Creating sustainable corporations. *Business Strategy and the Environment, 4,* 154-165.

Smith, A. (1937). An inquiry into the nature and causes of the wealth of nations. In M. Lerner & E. Canaan (Eds.), *An Inquiry Into The Nature And Causes Of The Wealth Of Nations.* New York, NY: The Modern Library. (Original work published 1789)

Smith, A. (1982). The theory of moral sentiments. In D. D. Raphael & A. L. Macfie (Eds.), *The theory of moral sentiments.* Indianapolis, IN: Liberty Press/Liberty Classics. (Original work published 1790)

Smith, R. A. (1996). Leadership as aesthetic process. *Journal of Aesthetic Education, 30*(4), 39-52.

Spence, L. J. (2012, August 3). *Primer: Business Sustainability For Small And Medium Enterprises (Smes).* Retrieved from http://nbs.net/knowledge/primer-business-sustainability-for-smes/

Starik, M., & Rands, G. P. (1995). Weaving an integrated Web: Multilevel and multisystem perspectives of ecologically sustainable organizations. *Academy of Management Review, 20*(4), 908-935.

Strati, A. (1992). Aesthetic understanding of organizational life. *Academy of Management Review, 17*(3), 568-581.

Strati, A. (1996). Organizations viewed through the lens of aesthetics. *Organization, 3*(2), 209-218.

Strati, A. (2010). Aesthetic understanding of work and organizaitonal life: Approaches and research developments. *Sociology Compass, 4*(10), 880-893.

Stubbs, W., & Cocklin, C. (2008). Conceptualizing a sustainability business model. *Organization & Environment, 21*(2), 103-107.

Suekane, A. (2010). *An analysis on long standing companies in Japan: Why they can be sustainable?* Retrieved from http://management.kochi-tech.ac.jp/PDF/ssms2009/sms09_144.pdf

Tainter, J. A. (1995). Sustainability of complex societies. *Futures, 27*(4), 397-407.

Tainter, J. A. (1996). Complexity, problem solving, and sustainable societies. In *Getting down to earth: Practical applications of ecological economics.* Washington, DC: Island Press.

Tainter, J. A. (2003, September). *The development of social complexity: Models of collapse, resiliency, and sustainability.* Paper presented at The Stockholm Seminars: Frontiers in Sustainability Science and Policy. Stockholm, Sweden.

Tainter, J. A. (2006). Social complexity and sustainability. *Ecological Complexity, 3,* 91-103.

Tata, R., Hart, S. L., Sharma, A., & Sarkar, C. (2013). Why making money is not enough. *MIT Sloan Management Review, 54*(4), 95-96.

Tay, L., & Diener, E. (2011). Needs and subjective well-being around the world. *Journal of Personality and Social Psychology, 101*(2), 354-365.

Taylor, S. S. (2002). Overcoming aesthetic muteness: Researching organizational members' aesthetic experience. *Human Relations, 55*(7), 821-840.

Taylor, S. S., & Hansen, H. (2005). Finding form: Looking at the field of organizational aesthetics. *Journal of Management Studies, 42*(6), 1211-1228.

TenHaken, V. (2008). Lessons learned from comparing survival behaviors of very old Japanese and American companies. *International Business & Economics Journal, 7*(1), 67-74.

TenHaken, V., & Cohen, E. (2007). Survival behaviors of 100-year-old west Michigan retail and service companies. *Journal of Business and Economics Research, 5*(8), 73-78.

TenHaken, V., & Kanda, M. (2006). Survival strategies of old Japanese companies and their effect on firm growth and profitability. *Proceedings of the Association for Global Business annual conference, 18,* 252-269.

Theis, T., & Tompkin, J. (Eds.). (2013). *Sustainability: A comprehensive foundation.* Houston, TX: Connexions Press. Retrieved from http://cnx.org/content/col11325/latest/

Tibbs, H. (2011). Changing cultural values and the transition to sustainability. *Journal of Futures Studies, 15*(3), 13-32.

Tokyo Chamber of Commerce and Industry. (2011). *Requirements for a permanent business: The lessons of enduring businesses to build the future.* Tokyo, Japan: Tokyo Chamber of Commerce and Industry.

Torelli, C. J., & Shavitt, S. (2010). Culture and concepts of power. *Journal of Personality and Social Psychology, 99*(4), 703-723.

Turner, L. (2013, June 7). *Seven Secrets Of Family-Owned Firms.* Retrieved from http://nbs.net/knowledge/seven-secrets-of-family-owned-firms/

Ulrich, R. S. (1991). Effects of interior design on wellness: Theory and recent scientific research. *Journal of Healthcare Design, 3,* 97-109.

Van Trijp, H. C. (Ed.). (2014). *Encouraging sustainable behavior: Psychology and the environment.* New York, NY: Psychology Press.

Veryzer, R. W. (1993). Aesthetic response and the influence of design principles on product preferences. *Advances in Consumer Research, 20,* 224-228.

Wasserman, V., & Frenkel, M. (2011). Organizational aesthetics: Caught between identity regulation and culture jamming. *Organization Science, 22*(2), 503-521.

Weick, K. E. (1979). *The social psychology of organizing* (2nd ed.). New York, NY: McGraw Hill.

Weiss, J., & Hughes, J. (2005). Want collaboration? Accept-and actively manage-conflict. *Harvard Business Review, 83*(3), 93-101.

Weitzel, W., & Jonsson, E. (1989). Decline in organizations: A literature integration and extension. *Administrative Science Quarterly, 34,* 91-109.

Wells, P. E. (2013). *Business models for sustainability.* Northampton, MA: Edward Elgar Publishing.

White, D. A. (1996). "It's working beautifully!" Philosophical reflections on aesthetics and organization theory. *Organization, 3*(2), 195-208.

Williams, S., & Schaefer, A. (2013). Small and medium-sized enterprises and sustainability: Managers' values and engagement with environmental and climate change issues. *Business Strategy and the Environment, 22.* doi:10.1002/bse.1740

Winston, A. (2009). *Green recovery: Get lean, get smart, and emerge from the downturn on top.* Boston, MA: Harvard Business Press.

Wrong, D. H. (2009). *Power: Its forms, bases, and uses.* New Brunswick, NJ: Transaction Publishers.

Young, W., & Tilley, F. (2006). Can businesses move beyond efficiency? The shift toward effectiveness and equity in the corporate sustainability debate. *Business Strategy and the Environment, 15,* 402-415.

Zaleznik, A. (1970). Power and politics in organizational life. *Harvard Business Review, 48*(3), 47-60.

Zimbardo, P., & Boyd, J. (2008). *The Time Paradox: The New Psychology Of Time That Will Change Your Life.* New York, NY: Simon & Schuster Inc.

Zokaei, K., Lovins, H. L., & Hines, P. (2014). Recapturing Monozukuri in Toyota's manufacturing ethos. *MIT Sloan Management Review, 55*(4).

Appendix A. Origins of The Thousand Year Model

Although the book centers on the example of the Nishiyama Keiunkan Onsen, additional data from the following companies were assessed to develop The Thousand Year Model:

Avedis Zildjian Company	Ibasen	Mellerio Dits Meller	Tanbaya
Bachman Funeral Home	Interface Inc.	Murate Gankyoho Chobei Shoten	Toyota Inc.
British Petroleum Inc.	International Business Machines (IBM)	New Britain Palm Oil	Uojyuu
C. Hoare & company	Jacquet Droz	Ounoya Shonten	Van Eeghen International B.V.
Confetti Mario Pelino	Jain Irrigation Systems	Patagonia Inc.	Villeroy & Boch
Echigoya	John Brooke & Sons	Poschinger Glasmanufaktur	Whole Foods Inc.
Edpya	Kokubu	R. Durtnell & Sons Ltd.	William Clark & Sons Ltd.
Eitaro Sohonpo	Kongo Gumi	Royal Dutch/Shell Inc.	Yamamoti Noriten

Fabbrica D'Armi Pietro Beretta	Kyoshindo Inazaki Hyoguten	Seigetsudo Honten	Yasuda Shokeido
Florida Ice & Farm	Levi Strauss Inc.	Sembikiya Sohonten	Young Electric Sign Company
Ginza Yoshinoya	Mannendo Honten	Shirley Plantation	Zhangzidao Fishery Group
Ginza-Akebono	Marchesi Antinori	Shree Cement	
Hoshi Ryokan	Matsumoto Trade Company	T. Anthony	
Hugel & Fils	Matuzaki Shoten	Tamasushi	

Appendix B. Exploring the Dynamics of The Thousand Year Model

The Thousand Year Model offers a management framework to address the seemingly intractable question of how to deploy power in order to achieve a competitive advantage through optimization of social, ecological, technological, and economic capital. This model has been assembled based on an analysis of the long-lived businesses shown in Appendix A, including Keiunkan, the longest-lived of them all. The model offers a framework for guiding leaders in their quest to optimize the different forms of capital through coordinating activities among each of the six areas of the model, which supports sustaining their business operations over time.

The Thousand Year Model also defines a framework for managing the dynamic forces that influence an organization's performance over time. These driving and restraining forces are in constant flux, and will shift in sometimes unexpected directions. The Thousand Year Model shows which forces are essential for long term success and viability, and how these forces can be harnessed to achieve long-term dynamic homeostasis.

By balancing these forces, we end up with an organization characterized by restrained growth, continual improvement of processes and systems, and full realization of the necessity of the survival of the company and its employees over time. The application of driving and restraining forces within The Thousand Year model, as well as the ways in which these forces are realized in each element of the model, are shown in Table 8.

Type of Force	Element	Means of Force Realization
Restraining	Control	• Adherence to standards • Conservative financial position • Focus on efficiency and profit • Anticipate and manage risks
Restraining	Commitment & Change	• Adherence to tradition • Formal governance structure • Limit organizational size • Modulated change • Defined leadership succession
Restraining	Integrity	• Focus on specific human needs • Provision of singular or synergistic satisfiers only • Alignment of credo, brand value, and customer experience • Maintain original brand identity
Driving	Relationships & Integration	• Co-create new solutions based on emerging social needs • Trust-based long term relationships • Positive company reputation • Restoration of impacted ecosystems

Driving	Mastery	• Positive and motivating organizational culture • Increased productivity from new knowledge and skills • Employee experienced meaningfulness and satisfaction • High employee retention
Driving	Learning	• Continual quality improvement • Ongoing technology experimentation • Constant innovation • Protection and enhancement of core technology

Table 14. Force Realization in the Model Elements

The Role of Leadership

A core job of the leaders within a sustainable company is to align the different management elements to achieve overall effectiveness. Although The Thousand Year Model provides an integrated framework for managing the concerns associated with a sustainable company, leaders must provide alignment among the different model elements, set management agendas and goal seeking behaviors, and move the company through time towards a meaningful destination. The role of leadership is absolutely essential for a sustainable company and for the implementation of any set of strategies based on The Thousand Year Model. Leadership is as vital to a sustainable company as sunshine is to a growing plant. Without leadership, a company will simply wither and die over time. Without strong organizational leadership, The Thousand Year Model does not provide adequate guidance for becoming sustainable. Yet, when we include leadership, the model comes alive with possibilities.

There is an important corollary to this approach: a company cannot manage its way to sustainability; it must be led. Without effective leadership, a company simply cannot develop the necessary integration, nor can it make sense of the changes needed to adapt to fluctuations in its operating environment. Without effective leadership, the company risks adopting the silo-based approach that has caused the demise of so many hierarchical organizations.

www.ingramcontent.com/pod-product-compliance
Lightning Source LLC
Chambersburg PA
CBHW050102210326
41519CB00015BA/3800